The Popular Background to Goethe's Hellenism

The Popular Background to Goethe's Hellenism

BY

HUMPHRY TREVELYAN

LONGMANS, GREEN AND CO.
LONDON · NEW YORK · TORONTO
1934

LONGMANS, GREEN AND CO. LTD.

39 PATERNOSTER ROW, LONDON, E.C. 4
6 OLD COURT HOUSE STREET, CALCUTTA
53 NICOL ROAD, BOMBAY
36A MOUNT ROAD, MADRAS

LONGMANS, GREEN AND CO.

114 FIFTH AVENUE, NEW YORK
221 EAST 20TH STREET, CHICAGO
88 TREMONT STREET, BOSTON

LONGMANS, GREEN AND CO.

480 UNIVERSITY AVENUE, TORONTO

Made in Great Britain

PREFATORY NOTE

I HAVE been asked to write a short foreword to this work of my former pupil Mr. Trevelyan, and I do so with great pleasure, since I consider it to be a most creditable and useful piece of work. Comparatively little is known about the genesis of the remarkable neo-Hellenic movement in German literature at the end of the eighteenth century, in spite of the large volume of criticism existing about that movement itself; and this book is an important contribution to the understanding of its remoter origins and the conditions from which it proceeded. In his analysis of those conditions Mr. Trevelyan goes a long way towards explaining some of the most curious features in the attitude of Goethe, Schiller, and others to Greek antiquity.

In the author's absence in Labrador it was necessary for others to read the proofs; and these others have thought it advisable, acting on their own responsibility, to translate all the German quotations except those in verse.

A. H. J. KNIGHT.

TRINITY COLLEGE, CAMBRIDGE.
January 1934.

CONTENTS

INTRODUCTION

For good or ill, Goethe could not get away from the Greeks. He took them, in the middle of his life, as models to be followed unquestioningly, even to the extent of reproducing their faults. He tried to imitate their way of life as well as their art. What he thought he was imitating was largely a figment of his own mind. He attributed to the Greeks the ideals which sprang intuitively from his own heart. Much that he attributed to Hellenism is indeed there, for despite his imperfect knowledge there were innate traits in his character which gave him an instinctive understanding of the Greeks. But this instinct was overlaid partly by other non-Greek traits, still more by ideas acquired during his early life. Some of these ideas are clear in their origin and their working ; they were due to the direct influence of Lessing, Oeser, Winckelmann and Herder. It would be interesting and profitable to trace the changes which Goethe's view of the Greeks suffered under the influence of these men, until it settled down in Italy to that conception on which all his "classical" writings were based. But some preliminary work is necessary, if the influence of Winckelmann and Herder is to be seen in its proper perspective. There is a subtle background to all direct influences, that invisibly determines the extent to which they take effect and the amount of distortion they suffer in the process: I mean the general tone of public opinion, the "atmosphere" in which we are brought up; that stock of common ideas, truths and fallacies jumbled irretrievably together, against which we may rebel if we like, but which nevertheless inevitably moulds all our ideas, often in the way we least suspect.

It is this preliminary work, the reconstruction of this "atmosphere," that I have attempted. The attempt cannot help but be three parts a failure, for "atmospheres," whether physical or historical, are volatile and unenduring. Unless a diligent Boswell is at hand the significant conversation escapes for ever and is soon forgotten. And it is chiefly in conversation that "atmospheres" reveal themselves. Something can still be learnt from books of the day; something can be deduced by more indirect means. In working out a method I have been enormously helped by the late Marshall Montgomery's most successful attempt to do the same for Hölderlin as I have wished to do for Goethe.[1] At times, indeed, it has been difficult not to follow Montgomery almost line for line. But the subject is large enough to allow of much difference of treatment.

I have tried to make it clear that in Goethe's youth public opinion in Germany was still shockingly ignorant of the Greeks, although not so ignorant as it had been in the previous generation; and that it was only just emerging from an attitude of extraordinary hostility to the ancient world. I have tried to give an idea of the new, appreciative attitude to the Greeks, which was developing in the late 'fifties

[1] *Friederich Hölderlin and the German Neo-Hellenic Movement* (Oxford University Press, 1923).

and 'sixties of the eighteenth century. Even then, though the attitude was no longer hostile, misconceptions were almost as rife as in the bad old days fifty years before.

I have deliberately left out of consideration those works which Goethe read soon after their publication and which had therefore had no time to affect the " atmosphere " before he read them. But there were many works, which had already affected the " atmosphere," before Goethe came under their direct influence, and these are pertinent to my enquiry. Thus I have discussed Winckelmann's *Gedanken über die Nachahmung der Griechen*, but not his *Geschichte der Kunst.* The former had been in circulation for twelve years before Goethe came to know it, the latter for only four. I have left Lessing and Herder entirely out of consideration for the same reason.

Wieland should also be excluded on this account : *Agathon*, *Musarion*, and *Die Grazien* all date from Goethe's Leipzig years. But Wieland was not like Lessing, Winckelmann and Herder. These were original thinkers, leaders of opinion, moulders of thought : Wieland merely reflected, with wonderful delicacy of detail, all the popular ideas and tendencies of the day. The easiest way to find out the " atmosphere " of the late 'sixties is to read Wieland.

My final conclusion is that there was no firm ground of popular tradition on which Goethe could stand while he was struggling to find his whereabouts in the ancient world. All was shifting sand. The old attitude of hostility existed side by side with an exaggerated enthusiasm, which took all manner of absurd forms owing to the general ignorance. In these circumstances it is natural, not merely that Goethe's conception of the Greeks had serious shortcomings, but that his effort to create a new Hellenistic philosophy of life met with so little popular success.

THE POPULAR BACKGROUND TO GOETHE'S HELLENISM

CHAPTER I

Knowledge of Greek Things in the General Public

A. *The Lean Years*

In Germany, as in the rest of Northern Europe, the sixteenth century had seen the rediscovery of classical antiquity and of the human and artistic values which it expressed. The desire to profit by this discovery and to assure its advantages to the nation for all time led to the foundation of new schools and Universities, especially in the Protestant parts of Germany, and to the reform of the older institutions. At its best the old Humanism was far more than a scholastic ideal ; it was a way of life, for which the ancients were the models. The business of the schools was to train the mind to this new way of life.

But inevitably, in the flux of human development, the idea died and left nothing but the husk. Already in the early seventeenth century nothing remained of the scholastic tradition of Humanism but the imitation of classical authors and its attendant load of grammar. The study of the ancients for their thought or the beauty of their works was no longer known.

The Humanistic ideal had yielded to the Christian; or rather the two ideals were no longer able to flourish side by side, marvellously enriching and strengthening each other, as they had done in the first generous burst of new life and strength.[1] Hellenism and Christianity stood in men's minds for two radically opposed standards of value. Christianity was in the ascendant, so Hellenism had to disappear. Comenius, a leader of scholastic thought in the middle of the century, would have no compromise with the pagan authors: "If we would really have Christian schools, we must get rid of the pagan teachers. . . . You say: 'Not all are foul (schmutzig): Cicero, Virgil, Horace and others are respectable and worthy.' I reply: These also are blind pagans, who entice the mind of the reader from the true God to gods and goddesses. God has said to His people: Think not of strange gods and let not their name pass your lips."[2] Greek was still taught and indeed encouraged by the Lutheran Church; but now solely that as many as possible might read the New Testament in the original tongue.

At the beginning of the century Demosthenes and Homer still occur in school curricula,[3] but even these finally disappear. The language of Sophocles and Plato was no more heard, except in its debased form on the lips of young theologians. It was even sacrilege to maintain that the Greek of the New Testament was a debased form at all. For how could an omniscient Deity write bad Greek?

[1] Zwingli, the Swiss reformer, wished to admit the great poets and sages of Hellas to the Christian Heaven. This was rather too much for Luther, but it was his active support which enabled Melanchthon to reorganise education in Protestant Germany on Humanistic lines.

[2] *Opera Didactica*, 1657.

[3] Paulsen, *Geschichte des gelehrten Unterrichts*, p. 319.

Paulsen gives one significant piece of evidence to show how suddenly and completely the interest in Greek ceased in the first years of the seventeenth century. He enumerates the editions of Greek authors which appeared between the Renaissance and 1800. The most important may be summarised as follows :[1]

Homer .	between	1525	and	1606 :	sixteen editions.
	,,	1606	,,	1759 :	one edition.
Sophocles	,,	1534	,,	1608 :	eight editions.
	,,	1608	,,	1786 :	none.
Euripides	,,	1537	,,	1599 :	six editions.
	,,	1599	,,	1778 :	none.
Pindar .	,,	1526	,,	1616 :	five editions.
	,,	1616	,,	1773 :	none.

Knowledge of the ancient world had withdrawn completely to the scholar's study. For the outside world the life and art of ancient Greece was henceforth a *Raritätenkasten*, from which writers and men of the world chose out quaint figures, names and pieces of knowledge, to lend grace or piquancy to their works. It was still so with Wieland.[2]

Orthodox Lutheranism had ousted true Humanism from the schools and Universities and made Greek the handmaid of theology. Christian hostility to Hellenism did not wane during the years that followed the peace of Westphalia, but rather took new strength, at the end of the seventeenth century, from the Pietist movement. But a still more formidable foe of the ancient learning appeared in an unexpected quarter. Descartes' rationalism, which was founded on the assertion of the individual's right to think and act for himself,

[1] Paulsen, *op. cit.*, p. 320.

[2] For an excellent summary of the situation which developed in the schools during the seventeenth century see Gericke's work on *Gesners und Herders Stellung in der Geschichte der Gymnasialpädagogik*, pp. 7 and 8.

had clearly points of view in common with Humanism, and indeed was its child. But children are, alas, sometimes ungrateful, and all too prone to despise their parents. The followers and admirers of Descartes, Hobbes and Leibnitz were no more ready to take their orders from the Greeks than from the Christian Church. Indeed in the days before they had plucked up courage openly to attack the Church, they found in the Greeks, already discredited by the Christians, a safe and easy target.[1]

To put the attitude of Rationalism towards Humanism more sympathetically: the Rationalists were strong Modernists; they were the first to conceive the possibility of modern man achieving such deeds in art and science as the ancients had achieved. Their eyes looked forwards to the goal of earthly perfection through Reason, and in the first flush of hope and confidence they were unjust to all that lay behind them. In the Querelle des Anciens et des Modernes, which raged most hotly in France, the general mass of opinion, despite conspicuous and brilliant exceptions, was on the side of the Moderns.

Besides Modernism, another tendency of Rationalism, which is perhaps more of its essence, was also unfavourable to the study of Greek—namely Utilitarianism. The Rationalists, in their eagerness to achieve the perfection of man, which they believed almost within their reach, concentrated their forces

[1] Descartes himself had no use for the Greeks. "Je m'étonne," he exclaimed one day on discovering Queen Christine engaged in a Greek lesson, "que Sa Majesté s'amuse à ces bagatelles. Pour moi j'en ai appris tout mon saoul dans le collège étant petit garçon ; mais je me sais bon gré d'avoir tout oublié quand je suis parvenu à l'âge de raisonnement" (Rigault, *Querelle des anciens et des modernes*, Paris, 1856, p. 49). Did the poor Queen sometimes wish Descartes had not come to quite such an "âge de raisonnement"?

only on such knowledge as seemed to them directly useful to their end : in this a proficiency in Greek could not reasonably be included. Modern studies of all sorts were introduced into the curricula of schools and Universities and drove out what was left of the teaching of Greek and much even of the instruction in Latin. Moreover, even those who were not so eager for the immediate perfection of mankind, but thought rather of their own success in the world, were encouraged by the utilitarian spirit of the times to concentrate on those studies which would help them most quickly to a post and an income. The ideal of a broad, many-coloured and generous culture was out of fashion.

The other great spiritual tendency of the time, Pietism, though so profoundly opposed to the new and all-conquering Rationalism, was in this respect curiously similar to it. The Pietists were equally loath to waste any precious moments on the mere ornaments of a widely humanist education—even supposing that they could have been brought to admit that such ornaments as Greek literature were not actually harmful and dangerous. In fact they were as bitterly opposed to humanistic ideals as their orthodox predecessors.

On general grounds then the prospects are small for finding the humanistic studies in schools and Universities any better off at the end of the century than they had been in the middle. And in fact the actual condition of affairs was in every way as bad as could be.

The new University of Halle, founded in 1696, which represented the concrete manifestation of the now well-established ideas that had been taking form in the last fifty years or more, combined for the first period of its existence both Pietistic and Rationalistic tendencies. It could therefore claim to represent the spirit of the age as fully as one institution could do.[1] The Theological Faculty was under the direction of the great Pietistic pedagogue Francke, who favoured "an exact knowledge of the two ancient languages," but only for strictly theological purposes.[2] The Legal Faculty, which shared with the Theological the position of most importance at the new University, was under the direction of Thomasius, the most active populariser of the new ideas of Descartes, Bacon and Leibnitz in Germany. Although belonging essentially to the Rationalistic school, Thomasius did not find it impossible to work in harmony with the Pietist Francke. They were at one particularly in their opposition to the Old Humanistic ideals and methods. The following utterance of Thomasius on the value of Greek literature in education would have won nothing but praise from his formidable colleague.

"Melanchthon," he wrote in a note to M. v. Osse's Testament,[3] "certainly deserved praise for introducing the Greek language. But he had not acted wisely in occupying the youth with the folly of the Greek orators and poets, and with the useless philosophy of Aristotle [the adjective is typical]. Why did he not have the New Testament or the Septuagint expounded in Greek lessons instead of Euripides, Sophocles, Homer, Aristotle, etc.? I should think the Book of Wisdom, of Judith, or the Maccabees would be as

[1] "Die Hochschule zu Halle war während des ersten Menschenalters ihrer Blüte . . . als die Vertreterin des Modernen auf den Plan erschienen" (Brode, *Die Friederichs-Universität zu Halle*, Halle, 1907, p. 21).

[2] Paulsen, *op. cit.*, p. 357.

[3] Paulsen, *op. cit.*, p. 360.

good or better than that fool (Narr) Homer and the other pagan poets and orators."

With the conduct of the new University essentially in the hands of these two men it is not surprising that classical studies made little progress. There was a Professor of Eloquence (as the Classical Professor was then usually called : a survival from the sixteenth century ideal of Latin and Greek scholarship), one Cellarius ; but as Paulsen says "he found little response" in Halle.[1] Cellarius tried to arouse interest for his Faculty by founding a Philological Seminar, but apparently without success. In his inaugural lecture he complained of the small numbers of the school, and attributed this to the fact that every one thought it a waste of time to learn about the Ancients, and would concentrate on nothing but their Fachstudien.[2]

Here is clear proof of the fatal effect on classical knowledge of the utilitarianism of the Aufklärung. The records of the University confirm Cellarius' words only too fully. Every student on his matriculation inscribed himself either in the Theological or in the Legal Faculty, since these alone led to a career. Many of the teachers themselves in the Philological Faculty were also teachers in one of the two principal Faculties.[3] We can well believe Cellarius' pupil and biographer, Burckhard, when he says : "Cellarius was nearly in despair over Greek."

In the older Universities the study of the Classics did not drop out so completely as at Halle. At Leipzig, Wittenberg and Tübingen, there was never a complete

[1] According to Justi (*Winckelmann und seine Zeitgenossen*, Vol. I. p. 52) his duties did not go beyond the teaching of Latin. The Professorship of Greek was combined with that of Oriental Languages. The Professors were Orientalists rather than Grecians.

[2] Paulsen, p. 358.

[3] *Ibid.*, p. 361.

break in the humanistic tradition.[1] But even at these Universities the value of the teaching was practically nothing. The Old Humanistic method forced down unwilling throats a meal of dusty bones under the name of ancient learning. Those who did not choke of it became as desiccated as the poison they had swallowed. Those Universities, such as Jena and Königsberg, where the New Testament was the only Greek read, were perhaps lucky. Even at Leipzig in the 'thirties, Greek was almost entirely neglected. Reiske described his experience there as a student in 1733 : " I read some Greek authors ; but I knew no teachers (for there were then no Greek lectures given), was not provided with the necessary books, was ignorant of grammar and unaware of the value and necessity of it, and so did not get very far. Greek authors, such as Demosthenes or Theocritus, were too hard for me. I had no one who could explain them to me, so I soon got tired of them and put them aside "—and took up Arabic instead.[2]

In 1718 the Rektor of the Hildburghäuser school, Burckhard, complained that Plato, Aristotle, Homer, Thucydides, Euripides were not known even by name to the majority of University students.[3] The last survivors of the Old Humanism had reason indeed to wring their hands. Some went so far as to predict the return of barbarism : " Lapporum et Finnorum lingua, Gothico et Longobardico sermoni in famelicis suis et nauseabundis libellis juridice Stoice *i.e.* incomte et inficete philosophantur," exclaimed J. B. Carpzow, in his inaugural lecture as Extraordinarius of Eloquence in Leipzig in 1748.[4] It is doubtful whether a general

[1] Paulsen, pp. 364–370.
[2] *Ibid.*, p. 414.
[3] *Ibid.*, p. 376.
[4] *Ibid.*, p. 377.

inability to write such refined Latin as Herr Extraordinarius Carpzow would really have had the sad results he feared ; the wisdom and beauty of the ancients was to find its way again to the hearts of the Germans, not through the old methods whose neglect Carpzow deplored, but through new ways more fitted to the times and to the men.

The general tendencies in the schools during this period were the same as those which prevailed in the Universities. The direct needs of the pupil in after life were taken more into consideration, so that modern studies of all sorts were brought into the curriculum : mathematics, geography, physics, history, political economy, French and German. Inevitably Greek and Latin suffered. But the condition of the ancient languages never became so desperate at the schools as at the Universities. The tendency of the Pietistic and Rationalistic reformers was rather to attempt to speed up the process of learning. Throughout the first half of the eighteenth century a number of editions of classical authors appeared with Latin notes and some German words given—precursors of our "Kelly's Keys." J. B. Carpzow was particularly active in this work, by which he no doubt hoped to stave off the advance of barbarism, and he was followed by C. Juncker of Dresden.[1] Boysen's *Acerra Philologica* (1715-1723), which may have been the Acerra mentioned by Goethe in *Dichtung und Wahrheit*, Bk. I, as the earliest source of his mythological knowledge,[2] contained, besides articles on mythology

[1] Bursian, *Geschichte der klassischen Philologie in Deutschland von den Anfängen bis zur Gegenwart*, Oldenburg, München und Leipzig, 1883, p. 375.

[2] See Hotzy, *Studium zu Goethe's mythologischen Quellen*, Wien, 1912, p. 8.

and all manner of classical subjects, explanations in German of certain difficult passages from classical authors.[1] There were also Hederich's *Reales Schullexicon* (1717), and his *Lexicon Mythologicum* (1724) and *Antiquitäten-Lexicon* (1742). These works concerned themselves more with the history and mythology of the ancients than with the language. Hederich's attitude to history is narrow and unimaginative, but his books were much used, for lack of anything better, by those who wanted Greek and Latin for something more than grammar.[2]

The chief centre of the reforming influences for the schools was Halle. The Pädagogium which grew up gradually under Francke's direction in the last years of the seventeenth century was the model of the new type of school. The greatest amount of time and energy was devoted to the attainment of "Gottseligkeit," but Latin was not far behind. It was still the most important branch of worldly knowledge. Greek, however, "stood quite in the background compared with Latin."[3] It was a voluntary subject, and the New Testament was practically the only text-book. The more advanced pupils were supposed to read some Demosthenes and Plutarch, but in fact this seems not to have happened.

Francke's influence was already very considerable in Prussia at the end of the seventeenth century. A number of new schools were founded, in which the ideas of the Halle group and of Francke in particular were put into practice: the Friederichswerder School in Berlin, the Friederichsschule in Frankfurt on the Oder, the Collegium Fridericianum in Königsberg

[1] Bursian, *op. cit.*, p. 373. [2] *Ibid.*, p. 374.
[3] Paulsen, *op. cit.*, p. 383.

(where Herder later taught) were all founded between 1680 and 1705, and all were under Rektors who either had been at Halle or were in touch with the Halle ideals.

Under Frederick William I Francke's influence became even greater, as he stood in close personal relationship to that strange autocrat and became practically his spiritual guide.[1] A number of Decrees dealing with the conduct of the *gelehrten Schulen* were issued between 1720 and 1740, from one of which we may quote a significant passage. "No one shall be admitted to the highest class of the great *Lateinschulen*, unless he can construe (exponieren) an easy classical author, such as Cornelius Nepos, wherever it may happen to be opened, making only occasional grammatical mistakes; no one shall be admitted *in primam Graecam* who has not at least the declensions and the regular verb at his command, and can also construe the first ten chapters of the New Testament."[2] Here is a definite indication of the standard of proficiency in Greek, which was expected of the best scholars of the best schools in Prussia. λύω is the summit of achievement in Grammar, and φέρω and ὁράω are wisely left undisturbed. And even in Germany the ideal laid down in a Verordnung is not always carried out in practice.

It is not necessary to pile any higher the monotonous heap of evidence for the neglect of classical studies and of Greek in particular in the schools of North Germany at this period. But two famous schools cannot be passed over without mention—the Thomasschule at Leipzig, and the Fürstenschule of St. Afra at Meissen, where Lessing learnt his Greek.

[1] Brode, *Die Friederichs-Univ. zu Halle*, Halle, 1907.
[2] Verordnung, Oct. 25, 1735, Paulsen, p. 391.

The Thomasschule had the honour to receive as Rektor in 1676 no less a person than Thomasius himself; and this energetic populariser of the new ideas at once laid before the Council proposals, which were accepted, for modernising the curriculum in accordance with the spirit of the times. They amounted, in effect, to the supersession of all classical authors by the New Testament, varied with late Roman Christian writers and scholar-poets of the sixteenth century.[1] One of the reasons given is that for students of Theology "greater practical use is to be expected" from this curriculum. When Gesner became Rektor of the Thomasschule, in 1730, he found these authors still in use.

The Fürstenschule of St. Afra at Meissen presents, during the first quarter of the eighteenth century, a typical case of modernisation. In 1700, General History and Geography were introduced, "for which a great demand was shown even among the boys." In 1718 a French master was appointed to the staff, through whose influence a Dancing and Fencing master followed. A teacher of Geometry was added in 1721, despite the protests of the Humanists, who thought too much time was already spent on Mathematics. In 1726 the new Rektor Martius expressed doubt, "how far it was advisable to push Greek nowadays." At the same time the Inspectors advised less reading of Greek poetry, "since only a very small minority incline their minds to poetry." The Konrektor Sillig held out for one Greek poet, but proposed instead of the long-winded Homer some moral poet such as Hesiod, Theognis (a curious choice), Possilius or Rhodomanus. These suggestions were

[1] For details see Paulsen, p. 395.

mostly embodied in the new Unterrichtsordnung of 1727.[1]

Nevertheless, the Old Humanism had by no means disappeared from the schools by the middle of the eighteenth century. Latin remained the chief subject in the majority of schools ; Greek always had been far behind Latin, and now, where it still existed at all, was at an even greater disadvantage. But even though classical studies were still pursued, we have no right to assume that the effect on the pupils was to produce any great love for the ancient world and its values. Despite the best efforts of the Pietists it is clear that Greek and Latin were still taught in the majority of schools on exactly the same methods as they had been ever since the sixteenth century—that is by constant practice in imitation of the style of classical models and by much learning of grammar by heart. Heyne, in his own description of his school days at Chemnitz,[2] says : " Teaching in school was just the old dull round [Schlendrian] : Latin vocabulary, exposition and exercises ; everything without any soul or sense." Very little, if any, attempt was made to read the ancient writers for what their works contained of wisdom and beauty, of interest or of humour. The result was that neither pupils nor teachers took any pleasure in their work. Classics became a hateful and meaningless drudgery, which the average pupil gave up only too gladly as soon as he left school and became his own master. J. M. Gesner, the pioneer of the New Humanism, which was to come, wrote in his *Kleinen deutschen*

[1] Paulsen, p. 398.

[2] Printed in Heeren's *Historische Schriften*, Vol. VI. " Chr. Gottl. Heyne biographisch dargestellt." Göttingen, 1823.

Schriften (p. 293), that the old method of teaching "was the cause of the implacable hatred which the great majority feel for all Latin books . . . ; so that they used their so-called freedom chiefly for the purpose of renouncing Latin and their school books for ever."

Undoubtedly the lack of interest in the classics was largely due to the badness of the teaching, to the faulty method, and not less to the ignorance of the teachers themselves. Paulsen [1] quotes Nicolai's own comment on his experience at the Halle Waisenhaus: after making a good start in Greek, he was so disgusted by a "howling pietistic pedant," who taught, of course, from the New Testament, that he gave it up altogether. Just before he left the school in 1747 he got to know a little of Homer out of Freyer's *Fasciculus Poematum Graecorum*, and says he would certainly have stayed in the Greek class, if this fasciculus had been recommended to him instead of the New Testament. He first learnt Greek properly ten years later, when he and Mendelssohn took lessons from Damm at Berlin, and read Homer together.[2]

Heyne had to struggle against discouragement as severe. "The New Testament and Plutarch 'On Education' were all the Greek books we knew [he speaks of the Lateinschule in his own town of Chemnitz]. In the top form I made the acquaintance of certain classical authors. Our Rektor, who had himself had Homer printed, gave private tuition on the rhapsodies. But he lacked in all things the very elements. So I got no taste even for Homer, read no single author through, and at my leaving the school, was quite unacquainted with everything connected

[1] Paulsen, p. 415. [2] *Über meine gelehrte Bildung*, p. 29 ff.

with classical scholarship."[1] Thus one of the great scholars of the future left school without so much as his interest being aroused in the classics. The schools were as good as useless.

In the realm of pure scholarship the lamp of classical knowledge flickered fitfully during these years, and cast its dim light chiefly into the dustiest and most deservedly forgotten corners of the ancient world. The best Greek scholar in Germany at the beginning of the eighteenth century was Fabricius (1668–1736), Master and Headmaster of Hamburg School (1699–1711), but even his record of activity can inspire little enthusiasm to-day. His great work was a *Bibliotheca Graeca* (published from 1705–28), a history of Greek literature in fourteen volumes based on careful study of the MSS. It was a work of immense industry and learning, utterly unsuited, and indeed not intended, for general use. The great classical writers from Homer to Isocrates are all dealt with in the first volume; what fills the other thirteen is best left to the imagination: presumably Alexandrians, Stoic philosophers, scholiasts and Early Fathers. Homer receives seven chapters of the first volume to himself: the first two deal with his life and his works (including the spurious and the lost); Chapters III, IV, and V consist of lists of scholiasts, commentators, translations, etc.; in Chapter VI Homer's importance as an authority in the ancient world (rather in the manner of the Bible in the modern) is discussed; and with an account in the seventh chapter of the imitations and parodies of Homer, Fabricius feels at last that all has been said. However great its merits as a work of

[1] Heyne's Biography in Heeren's *Hist. Schriften*, Vol. VI. p. 16.

scholarship, it is clear that the *Bibliotheca Graeca* can have done nothing to popularise the classics in Germany. But at least it was sounder scholarship than was then common in some more famous seats of learning than Hamburg : Fabricius brings a number of proofs to show that the letters of Phalaris were neither by Phalaris nor by Lucian. He also produced a *Bibliotheca Latina*, and a *Bibliotheca Antiquaria*, precursor of the modern dictionaries of antiquities, and a *Menologium*, a compilation of the names of the months which have come down from antiquity, showing great diligence but an insufficient knowledge of the facts." [1]

He also published with Latin translations certain obscure late Greek writers : Sextus Empiricus, Proclus of Marinos and Bishop Hippolytus. What more striking proof is needed of the disuse into which the reading of the great Greek writers had fallen than this spectacle of the best scholarship wasting itself in the sand ? Men were more concerned to hear a third-century Bishop's views on the Noetian heresy than Socrates and Phaedrus "talking of the passions of men."

Much time and energy was devoted to niggling and futile research into the way of life of the ancients. J. Nicolai of Tübingen and J. W. Berger of Wittenberg unbosomed themselves at length of their great knowledge on such questions as how the Greeks and Romans wore their gloves or their spurs.[2] C. G. Schwarz, Professor of Rhetoric at Altdorf, concentrated especially on their book-ornamentation and library-furniture.[3] The ancient world was still a *Raritätenkasten*,

[1] Bursian, *op. cit.*, p. 361. [2] *Ibid.*, p. 370.
[3] Montgomery, *Hölderlin*, p. 6.

into which now only the most hardened dryasdusts had the courage or the wish to penetrate. The best scholars were not interested in antiquity. At the new Berlin Academy (founded 1700) only one paper of any importance on a Greek subject was read between 1700 and 1743—by one Elsner, suggesting certain emendations in late Greek prose-writers, and containing notes on Greek and Latin inscriptions.[1] Sinology and Egyptology received more attention than classical antiquity.

Such a picture, however inadequately traced, of the almost complete collapse of humanistic studies in Germany at the beginning of the eighteenth century, is of interest in itself to anyone to whom the Greek genius represents a factor of constant value in the spiritual life of man. How did this collapse affect Goethe's early ideas and education on Greek matters?

Of ordinarily cultivated people whose schooling fell in the first forty years of the eighteenth century, very few indeed can have left school or University with any sort of real groundwork of classical knowledge. Interest in the Greeks, and even admiration for them, was not dead among cultivated men and women, but it must have lacked all solid basis of knowledge.

Those men who had influence on the development of Goethe's mind, either by personal contact or by the written word, were all at school and University precisely in the period when Greek scholarship was at its lowest point. Goethe's father was born in 1710; the years of his schooling, which he spent at the Coburg Gymnasium and Leipzig University, fell, therefore, roughly between 1720 and 1730. The

[1] Bursian, *op. cit.*, p. 359.

friends of his father, whom Goethe mentions in *Dichtung und Wahrheit*, von Uffenbach, von Häkel, his uncle von Loën, Dr. Orth, the three Ochsenstein brothers, the Senkenberg family, Karl von Moser, whom Goethe mentions especially as a mind of considerable influence in their circle—all these, whether younger or older than Goethe's father, must have suffered from the same disadvantages in their Greek education. And so in the most impressionable years of his boyhood Goethe can never have heard any well-informed discussion of Greek matters. If the grown-ups concerned themselves at all with the Greeks, the opinions they uttered were probably ignorant misconceptions and gross fallacies such as could not survive for a moment to-day.

B. *The Revival*

The unresting ebb and flow of human tastes and prejudices is a fascinating study to the historian. Can some causes, economic or social, always be traced for the passing of every enthusiasm and the growth of each new fashion? It may be so. But it is not my purpose to ask why the spirit of Hellas began once more to stir in men's hearts. It had to come, as surely as the sun must return after the night. I can only trace the stages by which it strove and conquered.

The first signs of a reviving interest in the Greeks appeared in the schools, and here the greatest enemies of Hellenism had prepared the way for its easy advance. The Pietists had swept away not merely the substance of the Old Humanism, but its method and pedagogic ideals as well, and had substituted more living ideals and a more efficient method. The first teachers of the New Humanism took over the Pietists' technique and that part of their ideals which regarded education as a training for life, not a system for cramming young minds as tight as they would hold with useless knowledge.

The successful battle waged against the Old Humanist methods by Pietists and Rationalists alike made it easy for the real understanding and love of the Greeks, which the New Humanists preached, to spread through all strata of educated society.

The first of these New Humanists was J. M. Gesner (1691–1761). If any date can be given to the beginning of the new movement, it must be the year of Gesner's appointment as Rektor of the Thomasschule in Leipzig (1730). By 1740 we can reckon the movement as well started—Gesner's ideas were increasingly recognised as the up-to-date tendency in education, though they were still far from being generally accepted or put into practice throughout Germany.

Gesner's views on the teaching of Greek, which express the attitude of the coming generation to the ancient writers, are contained in a number of different works: in the new Schulordnung, which he drew up for the Brunswick schools in 1737 (this is the fullest and most connected exposition); in a collection of smaller *Gelegenheitsschriften*, which appeared in his *Kleinen deutschen Schriften* (Göttingen 1756), and in the *Isagoge in eruditionem universalem* (Leipzig 1757), which Goethe mentions in *Dichtung und Wahrheit* (II, bk. 6). His fundamental principle was that the ancient authors were to be read for their content, for the wisdom of their thoughts and for the beauty of the form and expression which they gave to those thoughts, so that the pupil's mind and taste should be trained by a loving study of the greatest works of literature and philosophy. It was to be a training for life in the highest sense, a training of the mind and spirit to understand and judge the values of the world, so that in any circumstances the man should "have full knowledge of the right road": it was to be neither impossibly "ideal," out of touch with all worldly values and requirements, as the Old Humanism had become, nor narrowly utilitarian like the Halle Rationalism, which taught only for the immediate need of obtaining a material livelihood. And it was to be something more than a training for life; for the gifted few at least it was to lead them to creative effort of their own, in literature, in philosophy and in art, and no longer, as the Old Humanists had vainly attempted, to composition in the ancient languages—the day of such delusions was long past—but to the vigorous and refined use of the mother tongue.[1] Could Gesner have lived to read *Hermann und Dorothea*, he would have felt that his seedling had borne golden fruit.

The chief obstacle which Gesner had to overcome was the general disrepute into which the great men of Greece and Rome had fallen. The first necessity was to re-establish a favourable attitude towards the ancients in the mind of the pupil. In the Schulordnung (§ 97) he writes : "The teacher will be particular to give the young people a good opinion of the ancients in general and of the pleasure and use of being well read in them. He should say to them that most of the ancient writers were the most excellent people of their time, and wrote not from any unworthy motives, but simply and solely that they might leave to posterity a perpetual memorial of reason and other good qualities. Whoever, therefore, reads and understands their writings, enjoys the society of the greatest men and the noblest souls who have ever been, and thus imbibes beautiful thoughts and words of weight, as always happens in conversation." It was time indeed that those hard words of Comenius should be recanted, nor could the great dead demand a fairer recantation.

If the primary difficulty, the disrepute into which the classical writers had fallen, was due mainly to tendencies which had arisen in the past hundred years, the second great difficulty, the impossible method of teaching the classics, was, as we know, of even older standing. The methods and ideals of the Old

[1] Paulsen, pp. 428 and 433.

Humanism were in practice a more formidable and tenacious hindrance to the spread of classical knowledge than the ideals of Pietism, which were now fast on the wane, or of Rationalism, which was beginning to look more tolerantly on the men of old days.

In the preface to his edition of Livy (1743) Gesner attacks most strongly the old method of reading an author. Everything, he complains, is read over and over again (in order that the words and phrases may be impressed on the pupil's mind for future use in orations or verses), so that in a whole year only one book of Cæsar or one play of Terence is completed. At the end of the year the pupil is quite unable to say what he has read. Of the content, the form and the beauty of the whole, he has no conception. While reading Homer or Vergil he has had but one feeling—boredom.[1] Instead, everything should be read quickly through so that the pupil enjoys and understands what he is reading. "The teacher's business is to focus attention constantly on the meaning. What would the author be at? What are his methods? How does he meet objections? How use examples, similes or evidence, either for ornament or explanation?"

In order to remove one of the great practical difficulties to his ideal of an education founded on a wide and appreciative reading of Greek literature, Gesner published his *Chrestomathia Graeca* in 1731. This book contained "selections" from the easier Greek authors, in particular Herodotus, Xenophon, Thucydides, Theophrastus, Aristotle, Plutarch. Its object was to

[1] See one of Georg Brandes' (b. 1719) letters to Heyne, July 21, 1766 (Heeren, *Historische Schriften, Bd.* VI, p. 137): "Ich habe es bisher nicht gewagt zu bekennen, dass mich Virgil nur an wenig Orten gerührt habe. Ich las ihn vor ein paar Jahren vielleicht zum zehnten Male, um mich zu prüfen, ob mich nicht etwa *der Ekel von den Schulstunden* her gegen ihn kaltsinnig gemacht hätte?"

enable pupils at schools and Universities to make the acquaintance of a number of Greek authors at small cost in money and shelf-space. For the only editions of Greek authors at the time were the complete editions, mostly brought out by the great scholars of the sixteenth century; there were no editions of single works.[1] The *Chrestomathia* was an economic proposition and fulfilled fairly well the demand of the New Humanism for wide, not scholarly, reading.

Yet perhaps the most striking thing about this book, the publication of which was certainly the first great event in the revival of Greek knowledge, is its omissions. There is not a single poet among the selections. Pindar we should hardly expect, the hardest of all Greek poets, and the Tragedians too are admittedly not easy. But Homer! That even Homer should be thought too hard, is significant indeed. There was no other reason for this omission than that the standard of Greek knowledge in schools was too low at the time. This can be gathered from the *Isagoge*.[2] "An ab Homero incipiendum?" Gesner there wistfully asks. "Affirmarem et hoc, si per extremas rationes posset fieri. An a Novo Testamento? Malim a narrationibus Xenophonteis et sermonibus Epicteti apud Arreanum. *Ut nunc est incipiendum a Novo Testamento*." The chief difficulty was that the teachers themselves knew no other Greek than that of the Gospels and the Epistles.

The task that lay before Gesner, when in 1730 he came to the Thomasschule from a post as Conrektor at Weimar, was a formidable one: the material on which, and with which, he had to work was so pitifully

[1] Paulsen, *op. cit.*, p. 438.
[2] See Montgomery, *op. cit.*, p. 16.

poor, and the result at which he aimed was so considerable. The Thomasschule was at that moment in low water owing to the incompetence of the deceased Rektor, Johann Heinrich Ernesti. Latin, for instance, was partly entrusted to the school organist, Johann Sebastian Bach, who, it may be assumed, had more important matters to think of.[1] Gesner soon set to work to reform the school, and in particular to reintroduce the reading of classical authors, who had been banished from the curriculum—with the exception of the innocuous Nepos—by Thomasius.[2] He at once put into practice his principle of rapid reading—with a comedy of Terence. But when he tried to do the same with the Phœnissae, the attempt broke down on the boys' sheer ignorance of the Greek language.[3]

The Thomasschule was for Gesner only a brief preparation for a far more important position, whence he was to influence the whole spiritual life of Germany. In 1734 he was called to the newly-founded University of Göttingen as Professor of Eloquence. As a generation earlier the ideas of the Aufklärung had been represented by the new University of Halle, so now the reaction against Pietism and the rise of the New Humanism was typified by the Hanoverian University. Theology was not encouraged: the new foundation specialised in "modern" studies; but one of the chief amongst these was "Philologie," which consisted very largely of Latin and Greek language and literature. From the outset it was intended that the

[1] With Gesner's coming he was relieved of this uncongenial duty, and allowed to devote all his energy to music: the curious may find a vigorous and admiring description of his playing in Gesner's introduction to his edition of *Quintilian*.

[2] Montgomery, *op. cit.*, p. 12.

[3] Paulsen, *op. cit.*, p. 434.

complete " modern " man should be equipped with a proper knowledge of the ancients.

The ideals of the new University were, in fact, precisely those which we have already quoted from Gesner's writings. " The Classics flourished in Göttingen. The aim was here no longer the imitation of Latin literature, but the provision of an æsthetic and literary education which should lead to an historical understanding of antiquity." [1]

As in the case of Halle, Göttingen became the centre for the spread of the new ideas in the schools and Universities of North Germany. And this was above all due to Gesner's efforts to train a younger generation of competent and conscientious schoolmasters, not pure scholars, who would carry on his work. On this part of his life's activity rests his chief claim to his countrymen's gratitude. To this end he started in 1738 his *Philologisches Seminar*. Greek was one of the most important subjects, and yet it is plain that even here, in the special class of the University, he was terribly hampered simply by the backwardness of his pupils. Here too " incipiendum a Novo Testamento " ; then, as mastery of grammar proceeds, his own *Chrestomathia* can be used.[2] He counted himself lucky if there was time before the year was up to read some Homer or some other Greek poet. Homer was, in fact, read in the winter of 1739, and then at frequent intervals. Now and then Sophocles, Euripides and Aristophanes were attempted. In 1760, the year before Gesner's death, the standard had risen so much that Pindar could be read.[3]

In 1757 he published his *Isagoge*, which can best

[1] Karl Remme, *Die Hochschulen Deutschlands*, Berlin, 1926, p. 7.
[2] Schulordnung, p. 27.
[3] Paulsen, *op. cit.*, p. 440.

be described as his Seminar lectures in note form. It contains a discussion of the best method of studying and teaching Latin and Greek, and deals with many aspects of the literature, philosophy and history of the ancients, and to some extent with their art. Goethe, as a boy, learnt mythology out of it (see *Dichtung und Wahrheit*, Bk. VI). By its publication the knowledge and ideas, which for twenty years had been given only to his Seminar, were made available to the public.

In 1761 Gesner died and was succeeded in 1763 by Christian Gottlob Heyne. If, even at the end of Gesner's twenty-seven years' work, the New Humanism as a great social and literary force was still only in promise, Heyne, in the forty-six years during which he occupied the chair of Eloquence at Göttingen, was to see it flower and fruit, and wither again in the mists of the Romantic Movement. And it was he, more than any other pure scholar and academician (for Lessing and Herder for all their learning were much more than this), who laid a foundation of living knowledge in men's minds on which a real and true understanding of the Greeks could grow.

For Goethe, Heyne's work at Göttingen came just too late. If indeed he had been allowed to go to Göttingen as he had wished, to sit at Heyne's feet,[1] his whole conception of the Greeks might have been different—sounder probably, as based on a fuller and more systematic knowledge of their history and art. As it is, Heyne's teaching cannot have produced any general improvement in the standard of classical knowledge in educated society in time to have affected Goethe to any important extent, before his conception

[1] *Dichtung und Wahrheit* II, Bk. VI.

of classical art was determined once for all by his journey to Italy. Yet as evidence of the new attitude of educated society and of "der studierenden Jugend" in particular to the Greeks during the 'sixties and 'seventies, Heyne's work is of great interest to us. The "atmosphere" can be gauged with some accuracy by examining what Heyne thought it worth while to offer his pupils.

Heyne carried on Gesner's tradition, and developed it. While Gesner's lectures were attended almost entirely by men who meant to teach the Classics in schools and Universities, Heyne lectured to large classes composed for the most part of men who were reading the Classics purely for their general interest. While Gesner had read chiefly prose authors, Heyne concentrated on the Greek poets. Indeed he saw the whole of antiquity essentially from a poetical standpoint.[1] It was the period when the true function of poetry was beginning again to be understood. Like all great spiritual leaders Heyne half went ahead of his time, half reflected its most typical characteristics. His *privatissima* on Homer and Pindar were attended especially by what one may call the non-professional or truly "amateur" students of Greek. Yet all these changes did not take place at once. When he first succeeded Gesner, as Heeren says, the Classics were "studied neither for daily bread nor from inclination." It was only with the lapse of years, as the times became more favourable and as he built up his own reputation, that his full influence began to be felt.

Typical of his "poetical" conception of antiquity and of his awareness of modern tendencies is his treatment of Mythology, which became in his hands one

[1] Heeren, *Historische Schriften*, VI, p. 163.

of the most important branches of the classical curriculum. Heeren says : " It was indeed the foundation of his whole outlook upon antiquity." [1] This assertion may seem exaggerated, until it is realised how Heyne looked at Mythology. He saw that with the Greeks the myths were not mere poetic fancies, invented simply to adorn the verse, but were the very essence of the poetry and life of the people, the Sagas of the half primitive Volk.[2] By thus ranging Greek mythology with the rest of the then fashionable folk-poetries, he probably saved it from suffering a severe eclipse in the reaction against the Rococo. Herder's influence was later the most powerful force in this matter, yet Heeren is probably justified in saying : " It is Heyne who deserves praise for having first applied this idea to antiquity." [3] Heyne was occupied with mythology from his earliest days at Göttingen : his very first lecture was on this subject. But his conception of the origin and poetic function of the Greek myths was not given to the world at large in any coherent form until 1782, when he discussed the subject fully in the foreword to his edition of Apollodorus.

His lectures on Greek literature were marked by that systematic thoroughness of treatment which was typical of him, and which was so greatly needed at a time when public enthusiasm for the Greeks in general sadly outran knowledge.[4] Again the question occurs :

[1] *Op cit.*, p. 167.

[2] An astounding advance since the days of Schulze, Professor of Eloquence at Halle, 1732–44, who, entirely ignorant of the Greek theocracy, regarded polytheism as invented by the Romans for reasons of political expediency, and read into the myths now chemical allegories, now " spinozistische Geheimlehren " (Justi, *Winckelmann*, Vol. I, p. 54). See Kont's *Lessing et l'antiquité*, p. 43.

[3] *Op. cit.*, p. 168.

[4] For details see Heeren, *op. cit.*, p. 211, and Paulsen, *op. cit.*, p. 441.

how different might not Goethe's view of the Greeks have been had he learnt systematically all that Heyne could teach him of their history and literature. He more than anyone perhaps suffered from an excess of enthusiasm and from the lack of a coherent picture founded on real knowledge.

The plan of Heyne's lectures on Greek Antiquities was equally methodical. Beginning with the geography, he dealt next with the history of Greece as a whole, and then with the individual states; the religion, games, methods of war, and finally the private life of the Greeks, concluded the course. If Goethe had heard Heyne, could he have insisted on regarding the Greeks unhistorically, as ideal creatures beyond the common chance of life?[1]

One more course of Heyne's lectures must be mentioned, for it is perhaps the most significant of the new spirit that was abroad. He gave one Kollegium on "die Antike" (beginning in 1767), in which he dealt primarily with ancient art. It was attended largely by young gentlemen of good family, and was particularly designed to help those who hoped to travel in Italy. Heyne first discussed the principles of æsthetics and then passed to an historical account of the art of the ancient civilisations, using Winckelmann's *Geschichte der Kunst* as a basis, and illustrating his words with engravings and casts of the more important works. In this way he hoped to train the taste and understanding of his pupils and to give them a groundwork of technical knowledge on which to base their judgments. It was a fine example of real scholarship and knowledge used so as to educate "for life."

[1] *Cf.* Gundolf's *Goethe*, p. 304.

It was in Göttingen that the returning sun of Hellas sent out its earliest and strongest beams. But in other parts of Germany the dawn had begun to glimmer almost as early.

In Saxony the spirit of true Humanism—the loving study of the Classics for what they contained of beauty and truth—had never been quite lost. It is noteworthy how many of the founders of the New Humanism came either from the Universities of Leipzig or Jena—Gesner, Ernesti and J. F. Christ; Lessing and Heyne.

Next to Göttingen, Leipzig became the most active centre for the new ideas. In 1734 the Thomasschule received as Rektor in place of Gesner, Johann August Ernesti (1707–81), a pupil and follower of Gesner who carried on in every way the pioneer's tradition. His opinions on the theory and practice of teaching are contained chiefly in a number of school Addresses, and correspond precisely with those of Gesner.[1]

In 1742 Ernesti became Professor of Eloquence at the University, and so carried Gesner's ideas over into the wider and more influential sphere. Heyne, who matriculated in 1748, attended his lectures and acknowledges his debt in his autobiography. "The admirable brevity, the thoroughness and good arrangement of his lectures riveted my attention more and more."[2] And Heeren says, "Among his teachers he put Ernesti first." But Ernesti, despite the best intentions, lacked the imaginative intuition necessary for

[1] See especially the Address of 1738, entitled "Melius utiliusque Latinos auctores intelligere, quam probabiliter Latine scribere." In an Address of 1736 he complains that the teachers have too little first-hand knowledge and teach everything out of Thesauri and Lexica—out of Gruterus, Graevius and Gronovius—a gruesome trio!

[2] Heeren, *op. cit.*, p. 28.

real understanding of the Greeks.[1] His lectures on Archæology (published in 1760) were little more than a collection of notes on ancient works of art, etc., from ancient and modern writers, "a thin thread of guidance to the external knowledge of the writings and works of art of Antiquity." [2] In the preface to the published form he warns his readers not to go too deeply into artistic questions. To Goethe in Frankfurt he "seemed as a bright light," but on closer view disillusionment seems to have followed. Goethe only mentions having attended one lecture of Ernesti's on Cicero "de Oratore," and in that he was more confused than instructed.[3] But for all this Ernesti cannot be denied an important rôle in the revival of classical knowledge.

In 1734, eight years before Ernesti became Professor of Eloquence, a man of a different stamp had become Professor of Poetry. This was Johann Friederich Christ (1700–56). He prided himself on combining his scholarly life and interests with a refined, even gallant, manner. He had travelled in Italy, interested himself in all manner of subjects, especially the arts, and had a fine collection of engravings, coins and gems. He supplied what Ernesti could not give, the feeling for beauty and poetry which turns pure knowledge into a force for training the taste and widening the understanding. Lessing wrote in reference to him, just after leaving Leipzig in 1749, "Only such men as he can praise the ancients worthily and follow such great examples without embarrassment." [4]

From 1739 till his death in 1756, J. F. Christ lectured

[1] See Heeren, *op. cit.*, p. 31, for the shortcomings of his lectures on interpretation.

[2] Bursian, *op. cit.*, p. 403.

[3] *Dichtung und Wahrheit*, Bk. VI.

[4] See Schmidt, *Life of Lessing*, p. 44.

on Antiquities, not confining himself to texts and inscriptions, but dealing with the architecture, sculpture, painting, etc., of the ancients.[1] This was the first attempt in Germany to regard ancient monuments from an æsthetic, not as hitherto from a purely historical, point of view.[2] But his lectures were not well attended, and Heyne calls them "a mass of digressions of all sorts, containing however some excellent observations."[3] These lectures were published after his death in 1776, when there was more demand for such knowledge.

Gottsched was also at Leipzig during this period, and at the height of his prestige and influence. The essential matter of his lectures was published in his *Redekunst* and *Critische Dichtkunst*. The indications which we get from these works of his first-hand knowledge of the Greeks reveal ignorance rather than learning. He starts his *Redekunst* with an historical sketch of the growth of Oratory among the ancient peoples. As an attempt at a concise presentation of the main facts and tendencies it is, to say the least, meagre, at times even seriously confusing. Having for instance mentioned Themistocles, Gottsched continues: "Soon afterwards there came Alcibiades, Critias and Theramenes": in the next sentence he mentions Pericles as the greatest political orator of all. Even if one has sufficient charity to assume that Gottsched himself knew that Pericles was a generation older than Alcibiades, Theramenes and the gentle Critias, it must be admitted that an ignorant reader would receive precisely the opposite impression.

[1] Bursian, *op. cit.*, p. 405.
[2] See Justi, I, 378, and Kont, *op. cit.*, p. 28.
[3] Heeren, *op. cit.*, p. 28.

His summary of the development of Greek tragedy [1] is equally unsatisfactory. Aeschylus is mentioned merely as having introduced the second actor and therewith the dialogue. "Euripides found the stage in this condition, but Sophocles brought it to still greater perfection." Here again we must get the impression that Euripides was the earlier poet, that Sophocles marks the final stage in the development of Greek tragedy. Gottsched also informs his readers that Sophocles made the choruses refer more to the action of the drama, whereas before they had dealt with quite different subjects. The opposite was in fact the case. It is clear that Gottsched had no first-hand knowledge of Greek tragedy, and that most of what he wrote, or taught in his lectures, on the subject was quite valueless.

Gottsched's shortcomings make it clear that even men of learning and culture who pretended to admire the Greeks, lacked to an astonishing degree the foundation of mere knowledge, without which a true estimate of the Greek spirit is impossible. If Gottsched could live comfortably in this atmosphere of vague half knowledge, what was the atmosphere among the good Frankfurt burghers, with whom Goethe grew up?

The New Humanism spread slowly from Leipzig over the whole of Saxony. Heyne tells how in his last year at the Chemnitz school (1747-48) a new Konrektor came from Leipzig. "As he came from Ernesti's school he possessed knowledge of which we had never heard the like before." [2]

Prussia lagged much behind Saxony in the form and standard of classical teaching. But from the 'thirties

[1] *Critische Dichtkunst*, Part II, ch. 10.
[2] Heeren, *op. cit.*, p. 22.

until 1766, Christian Tobias Damm had been Rektor of the Kölnisches Gymnasium in Berlin. He was inspired with the same ideals as Gesner, though independently; he regarded the knowledge of Greek literature as of primary importance to the national culture, and he did what he could to spread a real knowledge and appreciation among the general public. Nevertheless, in 1735, when Winckelmann, then eighteen years old, spent a year at the Kölnisches Gymnasium in order to learn Greek, the new spirit had not advanced very far. Winckelmann found Damm himself intolerably pedantic. Only two hours a week were devoted to the reading of Homer and Herodian in the Prima. Otherwise Greek was learnt almost exclusively for theological purposes. Moreover the method of teaching in both Latin and Greek was still that of the Old Humanism.[1] Damm's chief importance lies in his constant championing of the Greek cause, particularly in his attachment to Homer, though it is doubtful how much real poetic appreciation he had: his idea of rendering Greek "simplicity" in his translation of 1771, was to write in a homely, colloquial style, which was in fact merely ludicrous.

The tide which was running strongly throughout North Germany when Goethe was a boy had still hardly lapped the walls of Frankfurt. There had never been a tradition of good classical teaching in the Frankfurt Gymnasium and the revival found uncongenial ground to work on.

In the sixteenth century a Lateinschule had been founded (1520), which undertook instruction in the Greek and Latin authors. By the end of the sixteenth

[1] See Justi's *Winckelmann und seine Zeitgenossen*, Vol. I, p. 30 ff.

century the petrefaction, typical of the Old Humanistic methods, had set in. In the words of H. Voelcker,[1] that system was adopted which "set the linguistic form of the ancient classics above their intellectual content." This continued far on into the eighteenth century. In Greek sufficient grammar was taught to enable the pupils to read the New Testament and some prose writers.

The school was in a bad way throughout the greater part of the eighteenth century. The best Frankfurt families were not satisfied with the teaching available, and sent their sons away to schools of good repute in other towns, or provided them with private tuition.[2] Goethe's father went to the Coburg Gymnasium; Goethe himself, as we know from *Dichtung und Wahrheit,* had private teachers or was instructed by his father. In 1728 the Konsistorium of the school had resolved to attempt to stop this practice and to induce the burghers to send their sons to the local school, but with little success.[3] It is interesting to note that Goethe's grandfather, Textor, was on this Konsistorium: apparently neither family nor civic piety could induce Johann Caspar Goethe to entrust his son's education to the Frankfurt Gymnasium.

We may deduce something of the state of Greek teaching in the school from the account given in Voelcker's book of the Rektors in the eighteenth century. From 1717–22, a certain J. J. Schudt was Rektor, an Orientalist, who, however, published a Greek reading book. In the years before Goethe's birth the school was under J. Klumpf's Rektorship. He had the reputation of being a fine Greek scholar,

[1] *Die Stadt Goethes*, F.a.M., 1932, p. 149.
[2] Voelcker, *op. cit.*, p. 149. [3] *Ibid.*, p. 155.

and even tried his hand at writing Greek dramas. Perhaps during his Rektorship Greek studies may have been relatively flourishing, but we find no mention of any interest in Greek under his successor, J. G. Albrecht (1748–65), from whom Goethe learnt Hebrew, except that Goethe himself tells us in *Dichtung und Wahrheit* (Bk. IV), that Lucian was " almost the only author whom he read and valued."

In 1765 a new Schulordnung was drawn up for the school. It was modelled on Gesner's Schulordnung for Brunswick of 1737. So after thirty years the whole lump was beginning to be in some sort leavened.

Frankfurt was probably not exceptional among the towns of Germany in the backwardness of its schools. The schools in the cities, where there were no benevolent princelings to force through the acceptance of new ideas, retained the old bad ways far longer than the Landesschulen.[1] Even in 1780 Heyne wrote in the report on the Ilfelder Pädagogium, that there were but few of the Stadtschulen where an improvement had taken place ; the old teachers knew little Greek, and the pupils still had the idea that Greek was useful only to a theologian.

It necessarily took time for the results of Gesner's and Heyne's work, particularly in the training of teachers in the Seminar at Göttingen, to be felt in the schools of North Germany. Very few of Gesner's pupils seem to have become Rektoren much before 1770. In 1774 Schumann, one of Gesner's first pupils in the Seminar, became Rektor of the Hanover Lyceum. Ehlers, another pupil of Gesner's, went to Oldenburg as Rektor in 1768, and thence to Altona in 1771. The Darmstadt school was reorganised by

[1] Paulsen, *op. cit.*, p. 466.

Wenck, a pupil of Heyne's, in 1778. Three years before a new Schulordnung on Gesner's lines had been introduced in Hesse Cassel.[1]

Despite the great achievements of Gesner and Heyne at Göttingen, and to a less extent of Ernesti and Christ in Leipzig, the standard of classical knowledge in Germany during Goethe's youth and early manhood was still generally low. The will to learn and know about the Greeks was strong in the generation that was young with Goethe ; but owing to the abysmal depths to which Greek scholarship had sunk at the beginning of the century, it was sheerly impossible for all the seekers to be satisfied : the teachers were lacking, the tradition had all to be built up again, the background was largely false.

Goethe was born twenty years too early to enjoy properly the benefits of the revival of Humanism. When he was young, the knowledge which could have given him a more balanced perception of the Greeks was not yet absorbed into the intellectual atmosphere of cultured people. And since Goethe made no systematic efforts to acquire that knowledge, but contented himself with picking up what he could as he went along, and with bursts of reading, his views were strongly influenced by the ignorant conceptions current in the society in which he lived, rather than by true knowledge of the facts. It is true that from his Leipzig time onwards his view of the Greeks was chiefly influenced by such true experts as Winckelmann, Lessing and Herder. But it is precisely here that his own ignorance was most unfortunate in its results. Owing to the lack of a sheet anchor of sound knowledge, he allowed himself to be blown too easily

[1] Paulsen, *op. cit.*, p. 445.

first in one direction, then in another by the powerful blasts of these great, but individualistic thinkers. This might not have happened if the general standard of knowledge in society had been higher, and the average conception of the Greeks sounder and more trustworthy: he would then himself have unconsciously absorbed truer ideas, while the outstanding excellence of Herder's and Winckelmann's achievement would not have been so imperiously seductive.

C. *Art and Archæology*

It is almost beyond our power to conceive how Greek art must have seemed to people who were ignorant of the Parthenon sculptures, of the Hermes of Olympia and the charioteer of Delphi, and of all those lesser but not less lovely works which modern archæology has rescued from the creeping earth. Were Goethe young to-day, he would need only to cross the Main from his father's house to see one of the most exquisite figures of fifth-century sculpture, by Myron's own hand. In the Glyptothek at Munich now stands a more perfect group of typically Greek work than anything Winckelmann ever saw; while the masterpieces contained in foreign galleries are familiar to every schoolboy from photographs.

Goethe's contemporaries were less fortunate. In Germany, in the middle of the eighteenth century, there was practically no ancient sculpture to be seen—of genuine Greek work, probably none. The largest collection was at Dresden, but in Winckelmann's day it was still stowed away in a lean-to, unvisited and uncared for.[1] There were some antiques at Charlottenburg, of which Winckelmann, in his *Abhandlung von der Fähigkeit der Empfindung des Schönen*, says the best was an Achilles disguised as a girl. At Mannheim there was the collection of plaster-casts (including a complete Laocoön group and the Apollo Belvedere), which momentarily drove the image of the Strasburg Minster from Goethe's mind.[2] No doubt there were other collections of casts. But for

[1] Justi, Vol. I, p. 274.
[2] See *Dichtung und Wahrheit*, Weimar Ausgabe, 28.84 foll.

the most part those who were interested in ancient art confined themselves to the collection of gems and coins. Lippert's "Dactyliothek" was one of the most famous of such collections. The widespread interest in what seems to us such an insignificant sideline is proof that there were no opportunities for study of the great branches of art.

The systematic excavation of sites was only just beginning with the work at Herculaneum. Since the early years of the century there had been desultory digging,[1] and in 1738 it was taken in hand with more method. None of the results were published until 1748; the first official publication appeared in 1757. In 1780 the scene of chief activity changed from Herculaneum to Pompeii. But Greek studies naturally gained little from these excavations. Only Winckelmann was mad enough even to dream of digging in Greece itself.[2]

Before the appearance of Winckelmann's *Geschichte der Kunst des Altertums*, in 1763, nothing had been done in Germany to instruct the public on the subject of Greek art[3] except by J. F. Christ's lectures at Leipzig. The only published works of value were of foreign origin. The most important of these were Montfaucon's *L'Antiquité expliquée*, first published in 1719, of which a short version appeared in German in 1757, and the Comte de Caylus' great work, the *Recueils d'Antiquité*, the publication of which began in 1752 and continued until 1767, the year before Winckelmann's death.

[1] See *Historical MSS. Commission, Portland*, Vol. IV, p. 672. Letter from Alexander Cunningham to Harley.

[2] See *Geschichte der Kunst*, Book VIII, Ch. 3, § 20.

[3] See Stark, *Handbuch der Archäologie der Kunst*, for German archæology before Winckelmann.

But both these works had certain drawbacks. Montfaucon was not greatly interested in Greek art. The plates are chiefly illustrations to the text, which deals with the myths, the religion and the private life of the Greeks. No details of the originals of the plates are given—such as date, artist, size, material, etc. ; and the plates themselves are bad.[1] Not the rudiments of an historical treatment of the subject are to be seen ; no distinction is made even between Greek and Roman ways of life. *L'Antiquité expliquée* had a great success in France on its first appearance, and in Germany held its popularity into the nineteenth century. Winckelmann did not think much of it.[2]

Caylus was the first to treat the remains of Greek and Roman art from the æsthetic standpoint. Until then scholars had valued them solely for the evidence they provided on matters of history, mythology, or questions of everyday life, such as clothing, etc. Caylus himself says in the Avertissement to Vol. I, " Les Antiquaires . . . ne les ont regardés que comme le supplément et les preuves de l'histoire, ou comme les textes isolés, susceptibles des plus longs commentaires." For him, however, the monuments of antiquity are of interest because " ils mettent les progrès des Arts sous nos yeux, et servent de modèles à ceux qui les cultivent," and because they are " comme la preuve et l'expression du goût qui régnoit dans un siècle et dans un pays." At the end of the

[1] Stark says (*op. cit.*, p. 144) that Montfaucon reproduced drawings of the Parthenon frieze, which a Marquis de Nonteuil had had made. I cannot find these reproductions in the copy in the Cambridge University Library. There is a somewhat vague description of the pediment sculptures, and a miserable little engraving of the whole temple, obviously not from life.

[2] See *Geschichte der Kunst*, Vorrede, § 10.

Avertissement he expresses the hope that his work will lead artists back to the study of the antique, with its insistence on precision of workmanship and restraint of form. The introduction to the chapter on the Greeks in Vol. II contains a glowing eulogy of them for other virtues besides their excellence in art.

The chief disadvantage of Caylus' collection is that it deals only with works which the author himself possessed. These were for the most part statuettes, busts and gems. The only representation of one of the famous works of antiquity is an engraving in Vol. I of the Antinous, made from a small copy in bronze. Thus the reader got no information on the masterpieces of Greek art. Nor did Caylus make any attempt at chronological arrangement. It was Winckelmann who first made it possible to obtain a complete and ordered view of Greek art based on knowledge of the greatest masters.

But the *Recueils* had immense merit. For the first time the distinction was clearly made between Roman and Greek art, between Greek art and that of Egypt and Etruria. The engravings are of a quite exceptional fineness and excellence, and full details are given as to the origin, size, etc., of each work.

There were no other sources of importance from which a cultivated German could obtain knowledge of Greek art [1]—unless he went himself to Rome. Voyages to Greece seem to have been unthought of for Germans, although Englishmen were beginning to

[1] In the Introduction I have given my reasons for stopping short of the publication of Winckelmann's *Geschichte der Kunst.* It was this work which revolutionised the study of archæology and men's attitude to Greek art.

return thence with marvellous tales, and even accurate drawings, of what was to be found there.[1]

Montfaucon and Caylus, and the chance of seeing some cast of the Laocoön or the Apollo Belvedere—these were the opportunities which fell to the stay-at-home German to form an opinion on Greek art.

[1] There were four Englishmen in Athens in 1751, among them James Stuart, whose *Antiquities of Athens*, published in 1762, created such a stir in England, but seems to have been little known in Germany; and Robert Wood, whose *Essay on the Genius of Homer* Goethe reviewed for the *Frankfurter Gelehrter Anzeiger*.

D. *Mythology*

At the time when classical learning was at its lowest at schools and universities, Greek and Roman mythology continued to be used in literature, so that a certain acquaintance with the old fables was necessary for those who pretended to "culture."

At the time of Goethe's birth, the standard expected of the reader was not high. In Hagedorn's *Oden und Lieder* (1747) mythological allusions, if at all abstruse, are explained in footnotes. He finds it necessary to tell his readers that Achilles was son of the sea-goddess Thetis, and was educated by the Centaur, Chiron; that Calchas was a much-respected priest and seer of the Greeks[1]; and in fact to explain everything except such names as Minerva and Neptune.

In Hagedorn's poetry and in that of the Anacreontic poets, the use of mythological material is practically confined to a few stock figures, Jupiter, Minerva, the Graces, the Muses, and especially Venus or Cythera, Bacchus, and the pretty boy, unknown to Pindar and Sappho, sweet torment first of Meleager and the poets of the Anthology—Cupid or Amor, with his wings and his arrows.

In the fifteen or twenty years between Hagedorn and Wieland, the standard improved. But even Wieland never asked his readers to venture outside a fairly small circle of well-known myths. He expected an intimate previous knowledge of such tales as the Apple of Discord and the Judgment of Paris, and of most of Zeus' affairs. Such a form as the *Komischen Erzählungen* would be impossible if a previous

[1] Bk. II, *Die Helden.*

acquaintance with the story were not taken for granted ; the object is to re-tell a well-known tale in a new and piquant manner ; the whole would be impossibly heavy if every allusion had to be explained.

As examples of the standard expected by Wieland we may quote at random from the *Komischen Erzählungen* and from *Musarion.* Thus in " Endymion "[1] :

" Bloss weil er sie vom Wirbel bis zur Nasen
Im Bad erblickt, ward Aktaeon zum Hasen."

One would hardly guess from this that Actaeon was torn to pieces by his own hounds, but if one knew the story it would be enough to recall the fact. A very allusive passage occurs in *Das Urteil des Paris*[2] :

" Er stammte noch, der Streit, den Eris angeschürt,
Die Fehde, ohne die Fürst Priam unbezwungen,
Achilleus Zorn und Hektor unbesungen,
Herr Menelas am Vorhaupt ungeziert,
Und seine schöne Frau zu ihrer grössern Ehre
Uns unbekannt geblieben wäre."

Hagedorn would have filled a whole page with footnotes to explain this passage ; or rather he would never have attempted so allusive a style.

Musarion is packed full of allusions, from which we may select a couple :

" Sobald nicht mehr der goldne Regen rinnt,
Ist keine Danae—sobald im trocknen Becher
Der Wein versiegt, ist kein Patroklus mehr."

and

" So lief er auch—der weise Mann !—davon
Als ob ein Arimasp ihn jagte."

[1] Lines 132 and 133. [2] Lines 41 foll.

This allusion is unusually abstruse—but it would not greatly matter if occasionally a puzzled wrinkle appeared on the fair reader's brow ; it would all add to the piquancy.

Goethe, in his pre-Sesenheim poems, was at times more exacting than Wieland, though in general his use of mythological allusion is the same. In *Die Liebhaber* (*c.* 1766) the following very abstruse lines appear :

> " Da sank sie mit sterbenden Blicken
> . . . An meine hochfliegende Brust.
> So lag einst Vertumn und Pomone,
> Als er auf dem grünenden Throne
> Das sprödeste Mädchen bekehrt,
> Zuerst sie die Liebe gelehrt."

And probably not many of his readers recognised the Harpies under the name " Stymphaliden " in the *Ode an Herrn Professor Zachariae.*

For Wieland and the pre-Herder Goethe alike, Greek mythology and history were still a *Raritätenkasten*, from which they could choose pretty or quaint pictures to lend grace to their verses. It is outside the scope of this work to discuss how Goethe's attitude to the use of mythology had changed by the time he wrote the *Römischen Elegien.*

It is clear from these quotations that mythology never dropped out completely from society's stock of common ideas. Whence did the public get its knowledge ?—for there was no provision in the schools for mythological teaching. There were, even in those days, easy text-books for the general reader, written by men who generously desired to put their special knowledge at the service of the public. Some of these books attained to a considerable circulation. Mythology was the only subject connected with the ancient world which could be profitably treated before the middle of the eighteenth century.[1] Winckelmann's *Gedanken über die Nachahmung der Griechen* was a landmark in this respect as in others. By its subject matter it marks the new attitude to the Greeks as clearly as by its genuinely scholarly manner and its tone of unbounded admiration for everything Hellenic.

The majority of these mythological text-books were of an extreme antiquity—fifty, seventy, even a hundred years old ; they were still in general use for lack of anything more modern which could take their place. The actual information supplied by most of them was adequate for the needs of the public, whose wish was merely to be able to follow the mythological allusions in the poets of the day. But the spirit in which these works treat of the myths was very far indeed from that of the new Humanism of Gesner, Heyne and Winckelmann. They are full of the hostility and misunderstanding, whether Christian or Rationalist, of their time. The dead hand of the past lay heavy on Goethe's youth ; in this respect, as in others, the fruits of the new attitude to Hellenism were withheld from him until he came to Leipzig.

The most important of these earlier works were the two *Acerrae* (that by Lauremberg, first published in 1633 ; Boysen's, 1715–23)[2] and the *Pantheum*

[1] Anyone who wished to refresh his memory on a point of history or literature had to turn to some such school book as Hederich's *Reales Schullexicon* (Leipzig, 1717).

[2] It is not certain which of these *Acerrae* is the one mentioned by Goethe in *Dichtung und Wahrheit* (Bk. I, Weimar Ausgabe, 26.49). Hotzy (*Studium zu Gs. mythologischen Quellen*, p. 8) favours Lauremberg, but others back Boysen. The question is not of great importance.

Mythicum, written in Latin by a French Jesuit named Pomey, and first published in 1659. The two *Acerrae* were somewhat lacking in method, but they contained a deal of useful information.[1] Pomey's book divided the gods and heroes of the ancient world very systematically into classes, so that none escaped attention. It was brightly written in the form of question and answer between master and pupil, and was illustrated with quite passable engravings of the principal gods. It was deservedly the most popular of these books. A copy stands to-day in the small bookcase by the side of Goethe's desk in the upper room on the Hirschgraben.

The revival of classical learning had been in progress for some twenty years in the schools before the general public began to be supplied with new "popularisers." Until the middle of the century the seventeenth-century works held the field unchallenged. Then, in 1753, "a company of learned persons" in Frankfurt am Main published a *Neue Sammlung der merkwürdigsten Reisegeschichten* of the world in some thirty volumes. The Iliad was apparently considered to be one of these "most remarkable travellers' tales," for in the seventh volume a prose translation of it was given, made by Goethe's uncle Loën. From this translation, adorned with engravings in the "French theatre-style," Goethe first got to know Homer himself.[2] It was the first German translation of Homer since the sixteenth century.

But to us the contents of the previous volume are of even more interest than this translation, for it contains a very full account of Greek mythology, together with

[1] For Boysen's *Acerra* see Bursian, *op. cit.*, p. 373.
[2] *Dichtung und Wahrheit*, Bk. I, Weimar Ausgabe, 26.61.

a quasi-learned essay on the origin of the myths, their place in Greek religion, and the methods to be adopted in interpreting them.

It is safe to assume that young Wolfgang made himself as well acquainted with this volume as with that containing the translation of the Iliad. But it is of interest to us not only for the direct influence which it must have had on his earliest ideas, but still more for the evidence it gives of the classical "atmosphere" in Frankfurt in Goethe's youth, particularly in the society in which Goethe grew up. For though he tells us in *Dichtung und Wahrheit* that he hardly set eyes on his uncle Loën, the "learned persons" with whom Loën collaborated must, many of them, have been of the circle of the Herr Rat's friends, and known to Goethe as a boy.

The first part consists of a general discussion of the Greek myths, their origin, the proportion in them of truth and fiction, the means of interpreting them, the causes of the errors and superstition which they represent, and the reason why Homer thought fit to introduce them into his poems. All this is important only as an indication that, fifteen years before Heyne, the whole mythological question was exercising men's minds. But Loën's attitude to the myths is very different from Heyne's; to him they are still rather childish superstitions, used by the poets to adorn their verses with the requisite amount of "das Wunderbare."

The second part of the volume contains the myths themselves. The treatment is considerably fuller than in Pomey, although, as Maass[1] says, Pomey was probably one of Loën's chief sources. It is clear from his marginal references that he also used Hygin's

[1] *Goethe und die Antike*, p. 35.

Fabelbuch, a very full Latin collection, dating from the sixteenth century ; but there are often additions to the myths in Loën which do not appear in Hygin. Loën constantly gives marginal references to ancient authorities such as Strabo, Pausanias, Aulus Gellius, Athenaeus, and to poets, especially Ovid and Vergil, but this does not prove that he had read these authors : he could have copied the references out of Pomey. All the more usual myths are given ; all the gods, down even to fauns and satyrs, and all the major heroes are dealt with in a systematic arrangement modelled on the *Pantheum Mythicum*.

Mythology was the branch of classical knowledge which survived the lean years most successfully. But even its privileged position in the service of poetry did not save it from being treated with great indignity by the very people who purveyed it to the public. This ill-treatment is one of the most curious symptoms of the age, and provides an important clue to the mentality of the older generation.

CHAPTER II

The Attitude of the General Public

A. *Hostility to the Greeks in the Older Generation*

The most remarkable thing about Loën's handbook of mythology is its tone. He is not merely excessively fond of explaining away all the fantastic element in the myths; his whole attitude is one of contempt and hostility. He takes delight in belittling the heroes, in blackening the characters of the gods, and in pointing out the faults of the poets who made use of these stories in their works. He is not merely indifferent to the Greeks; he positively wishes them ill.

In the matter of interpretation he insists emphatically that there is always an historical basis of truth to every myth; it is only the ridiculous phantasy of poets and half-civilised peoples that has exaggerated them out of all recognition. Thus Prometheus did in fact exist. He was an astronomer who went much into the Caucasus to observe the stars. He wore himself out by his nightly vigils, and so arose the story of the vulture who daily devoured his liver. As for his having created men, it was simply that he civilised the Scythians—that is, made them into proper eighteenth-century *honnêtes hommes*, who are the only *men* properly speaking.

His rationalising ingenuity is not daunted even by the aeronautical feats of Daedalus and Icarus: they escaped from Crete in a boat like ordinary mortals ; they were said to have made themselves wings because they were the first to use sails ; Icarus tried to jump ashore too soon and so was drowned. Thus the exquisite symbol of man's courage, that falls blasted for its divine presumption, is reduced to a tale of commonplace mishap. O human Reason ! that would rob the world of all its beauty and pride itself upon the deed, and call it " progress " ! But even when Reason thought its final victory assured, the spirit of man was preparing to rise up against it and cast it out from its dominion over him. It had not many years more to deride and scorn the men of old time, because they lived in blessed ignorance of its yoke. The Genevan prophet was at the gates, telling already of its sure downfall ; and in Germany those men were boys who would laugh it as rudely from the scene as it had mocked the noblest spirits of old times.

Jupiter's success as a lover provided Loën with excellent opportunity for disparagement of the Greeks, and also for a sly dig at the princes of this world, a chance no burgher of the free city of Frankfurt could miss. For Jupiter, of course, was a king of Crete and died in that island at the remarkable age of one hundred and twenty years. Loën speaks with indignation of his " zaunlose Neigung zur Geilheit." " But what limits can be set to Might ? Such things can be seen even to-day among princes and potentates." A full list of his amatory exploits follows, and Loën sums up : " Such a lover was, therefore, exceedingly well suited to be the most exalted god of a licentious people."

The desire to paint the ancient heroes in the blackest colours is clearly visible in his account of the Atreid family. The story, as it is generally known, and as Goethe used it in *Iphigenie*, is not lurid enough for Loën. He adds to it such pleasant details as that Thyestes seduced Atreus' wife, that Atreus later married Thyestes' daughter (his own niece) who, however, was also raped by her own father, and had a son Aegisthus, who later killed Atreus, his mother's husband. Iphigeneia was apparently not the daughter of Agamemnon and Clytemnestra, but of Theseus and Helen, and was given out by Clytemnestra to be her own child in order to save her sister's name. The heroes whom the Greek poets used as material for their greatest works of genius are made out by Loën to have been nothing better than a set of the lewdest cut-throats. The inference is clear: what sort of poets were those who could be inspired to sing by such ruffians?

But Loën did not content himself with indirect attacks and insinuations. The character of Achilles, as painted by Homer, is in his opinion very far from satisfactory. Achilles' tendency to alternate tantrums and sulks is commented on with pain, and we are given to understand that the hero of the Greeks was not the model of an *honnête homme*. Having treated Hector's body with "a thousand indignities," he sold it back to Priam "for a great price"; which is indeed an accurate account of the facts. And yet the impression it gives of the motives and characters of Achilles and Priam is very different from what Homer succeeds in conveying in that incomparable scene in the twenty-third book of the Iliad.

But the passage of the Iliad which Loën found hardest to stomach was one which to our ideas stands out for its rare imaginative beauty—namely, the description of the Shield of Achilles. Try how he would he could not see how all the objects and scenes described by Homer could be made to fit into the limits of a shield. And how does Homer know what the lawsuit was about? For one can hardly suppose that Vulcan, who made the Shield, was like "those wretched scrawlers who when they draw a dog or a cat are obliged to write over them, "this is a cat" etc. Hardly, indeed! Loën feels that in making so serious a charge against Homer as this criticism involves—namely of writing something quite incompatible with the divine laws of Reason—he must have some authority of good standing to support his own, and names a certain "Herr Abt Terrasson," who had made special play with this objection. We shall have more to say of the Abbé Terrasson.

Loën grants that a M. Boivin has thought himself equal to all the difficulties put forward by Terrasson and others, and has worked out exactly how the Shield was arranged with measurements in inches. But the careful burgher of Frankfurt does not find M. Boivin's explanation entirely satisfactory. It is hardly surprising. Nevertheless, he appends a plate of the Shield of Achilles, "reconstructed" according to M. Boivin's measurements.

One sentence, from the account of Odysseus' wanderings, betrays Loën's whole attitude to Greek mythology and the great poems which grew out of it: "Here [in Phæacia] Homer puts the gods to quite unnecessary trouble in order to make the adventures of his hero, *which in any case have little value*, all the more marvellous." Then why, if the stories are all so valueless, if the gods were nothing but lascivious princes *à la Versailles*, if the heroes were a set of incestuous parricides, and Homer and the poets little better than idiots, why trouble us with an account of them? Would it not be better to ignore them and trust that an enlightened world will soon forget all about them? Perhaps, after all, a sneaking admiration for the old names lurked somewhere in the heart of the narrow old rationalist, though he dared not avow it to himself or to others.

The carping attitude of Loën was nothing new in handbooks of mythology, nor the tendency to explain away all beauty and delight that arises from the fantastic element. In Lauremberg's *Acerra*, for instance, the author breaks out suddenly: "Poets are regular liars. The names of the gods and all their goings-on are mere invented stuff." Pomey caps this with: "Mythorum causa prima est humanae mentis stulta perversitas," which was not an encouraging introduction to fairyland! The desire to see only the worst in the characters of the heroes comes out in Lauremberg too. "Others may be beautiful in body, but are ugly and contemptible in spirit, like Helen of Greece."

In Pomey we find the beginnings of Loën's rationalisation of the Prometheus myth. According to Pomey too Prometheus was an astronomer who watched the stars in the Caucasus until he wore himself out by his sleepless nights.

But Loën's hostility to the Greeks cannot be explained as the mere development of certain sentences and ideas inherited from the Pomeys and Laurembergs of the previous century. It is clearly the expression of a deeply-seated feeling, one facet of a *Weltanschauung*; and as Loën was not a particularly original thinker, it must have been a common attitude among the educated public of the time. It is a strange attitude in any case, and seems the more so when we remember that Loën's book was published only two years before Winckelmann's *Gedanken über die Nachahmung der Griechen.* Loën's attitude was a survival of ideas that had been current for seventy years or more, and which were about to disappear completely. But in Goethe's childhood they were still powerful and widely accepted.[1] To understand and appreciate them we must go back and trace them from their source, which lies in France in the previous century.

The Quarrel of the Ancients and Moderns

The Quarrel of the Ancients and Moderns is one of the most hackneyed subjects in the history of European literature. I intend not to give any detailed account of the course of the struggle, but merely to summarise the underlying ideas and to indicate briefly the attitude of those individual writers who are likely to have been read in Germany. An understanding of the situation in Germany is impossible unless this somewhat tedious digression is made, for as Montgomery says,[2] "By a dozen different paths every educated German, even to the very end of the eighteenth century, must have been led back to the French protagonists of the quarrel between *les Anciens* and *les Modernes.*"

The origin of the attack on the ancient writers was

[1] Perhaps particularly so in Frankfurt, where little was felt of the fresh breezes that blew around the courts of princes. For the backwardness of artistic taste in Frankfurt at this period see Adolf Feulner's interesting paper on Frankfurt artists, *Der junge G. und die Frankfurter Kunst,* F.a.M., 1932.

[2] *Op. cit.,* p. 115.

a healthy and justifiable desire among modern critics and authors to free modern literature from the cramping tutelage of the ancient models, to assert its right to develop in its own way and to be judged by standards arising out of modern conditions. But the champions of modern literature went too far. Not content with asserting the value of modern works, they came to deny any particular value to the works of the ancients ; and having established the right of modern works to be judged by modern standards, they went on to set up these standards as the absolute criteria by which to judge ancient works as well. The ancient poets had indeed little chance of being appreciated in a society whose habits of thought were in bondage to the Method of Descartes, and for which the only possible manner of life for civilised men was that practised at the court of Versailles.

Descartes' influence on the attitude of the Moderns is threefold. In the first place their rebellion against tradition is simply a transference of his action from the field of philosophy to that of literature. Secondly, his idea of Progress and the perfectibility of mankind led inevitably to a comfortable contempt for the ancients, as when the engineer of the Nile dam might watch with a patronising smile the efforts of children to check the flow of a brook with turf and stones. And thirdly, most insidious and far-reaching of all in its effects, the general rationalisation of men's mentality by the Cartesian Method destroyed all true appreciation of the essential poetical qualities in literature. Poetry became a form of geometry ; phantasy was not allowed to stray beyond the strictest limits ; those dark intuitions and visions, which scorn the approval of Reason, were treated with a pitying contempt. Thus men were incapable of appreciating those essential qualities of poetry and imagination in the ancient writers which justify and pay for all their faults. Lanson sums up: "Les adversaires des anciens, Perrault, Fontenelle, sont des cartésiens: ils appliquent à la littérature l'idée cartésienne du progrés, et ne voyant dans toute la poésie . . . que des œuvres de la raison essentiellement et nécessairement perfectible, ils déclarent les écrivains modernes supérieurs aux anciens.[1] Rigault speaks thus of Descartes' attitude to ancient literature and of his influence on later generations: "Il a voulu émanciper non seulement la philosophie, mais la littérature, et faire tomber . . . les liens qui unissaient l'esprit français à l'antiquité. Perrault est le fils de Descartes. Le cartésianisme, comme le cheval de bois des Grecs, portait dans ses flancs une troupe de modernes tout armés qui devaient, tôt ou tard, donner l'assaut à l'antique Ilion. Descartes, le premier, enseigna le mépris de l'antiquité.[2]

The earlier writers on the side of the moderns were concerned chiefly to prove from general theory that the ancients were unworthy of the exaggerated respect which they had till then enjoyed, that it was in fact impossible for them to produce such perfect works as the moderns, simply because the moderns had the advantage of all the material and experience which the ancients had been obliged to win laboriously, by a process of trial and error. The moderns start where the ancients left off. This crude idea, which in its rationalistic complacency leaves entirely out of account such imponderabilia as natural genius, was

[1] *Histoire de la littérature française*, p. 599.
[2] *Histoire de la querelle des anciens et des modernes*, Paris, 1856, p. 49.

first expressed by La Mothe le Vayer in a dialogue entitled Orasius Tubero.[1] "Il y en a qui déférent aux anciens," he says, "se laissent mener, comme les enfants, par la main de leurs pères ; les autres soutiennent que les anciens ayant été dans la jeunesse du monde, s'il y en a, c'est ceux qui vivent aujourdhui, lesquels sont véritablement les anciens et qui doivent par conséquent être les plus considérés."

Fontenelle expressed the same idea in his *Digression sur les anciens et sur les modernes.* (1688.) "Nous autres modernes, nous sommes supérieurs aux anciens ; car étant montés sur leurs épaules, nous voyons plus loin qu'eux." The *Digression* had, according to Rigault (p. 172), a great success at home and abroad. Perrault reduced the idea to its full absurdity in the first dialogue of his *Parallèles des anciens et des modernes* (1688–97) : the moderns must produce greater architects and sculptors, because they know more about geometry and anatomy, and have finer instruments and tools ! Yet even such absurdity passed for truth in the absurd Age of Reason. The mass of French society followed Perrault with delight, and took pleasure in looking down on the defenders of the ancients as a set of old-fashioned pedants.[2] The effect of Perrault's writings was not confined to France : in Germany it was almost more immediately felt than in the country of its origin.[3]

[1] Rigault attributes it to the year 1632, but there seems to be some doubt. See Rigault, *op. cit.*, p. 52, footnote.

[2] Rigault, *op. cit.* pp. 68, 157, 208 and 400, and Lanson, *Hist. de la lit. fr.*, p. 160.

[3] Rigault, *op. cit.*, p. 207. The easy victory of the Moderns with the general public is hardly surprising when it is remembered how few of those who were not professional scholars knew any Greek. The "general reader," if he wished to judge for himself, was driven to use translations which were for the most part the wretchedest travesties of the original ; or if they were good French, like Amyot,

The idea of Progress provided the Moderns with grounds, not merely for asserting the inevitable superiority of contemporary literature, but for denying practically all value to the works of the ancients. It was plain for instance, to any inhabitant of Versailles, that in social matters mankind had made quite immeasurable progress between the days of Agamemnon and those of Louis le Grand. Why, in the Iliad the nobles were not ashamed of losing their tempers in public, and actually cooked their own breakfasts! No one could expect a civilised human being to read descriptions of such grossness with any pleasure. It might not, indeed, be Homer's fault that he made his heroes behave so, since he could only paint from life as it was then, but at least let him no longer be held up to the admiration of men and women in an age which knew better how to behave!

The charge of *grossièreté* was repeated again and again, until Rousseau came and, with a wave of his wand, changed this blackest fault into a supreme virtue. One finds the same attitude in Fontenelle, in Perrault, in Bayle, in La Motte, and even, though much moderated, in Voltaire. In the poem on *Le Siècle de Louis le Grand*, with which, in 1687, Perrault declared war on the authority of the ancients, he blames the brutality of the heroes, and in the third volume of his *Parallèles* (p. 47) he writes: "Les

they were extremely free and inexact. A seventeenth-century translator thought it his right if not his duty to alter and "improve" the original as Dryden did with Chaucer and Shakespeare (Rigault, *op. cit.*, p. 61). De la Valterie, one of the few French translators of Homer before Mme. Dacier, watered away all the "grossièreté," and cut out as much as possible of the "longueurs." Mme. Dacier's translation of the *Iliad* (1699) was the first rendering of Homer to be carried out with a proper sense of responsibility to the original. In Germany there was no translation of Homer between the sixteenth century and Loën's *Iliad* in 1753.

mœurs [d'Homère] semblent ridicules par rapport à celles du temps où nous sommes ; comme de voir des Héros qui font eux-mêmes leur cuisine, et des Princesses qui vont laver la lessive." And two pages later : "Je suis offensé d'entendre Achille qui traite Agamemnon d'ivrogne et d'impudent, qui l'appelle sac-à-vin et visage de chien. Il n'est pas possible que des Roys et de grands Capitaines ayent jamais été assez brutaux pour en user ainsi ; ou si cela est arrivé quelquefois, ce sont des mœurs trop indécentes, pour être représentées dans un Poëme." "Je trouve Homère inexcusable dans ce caractère [of Achilles], qu'il a outré en mal, sans aucun besoin." La Motte, in his "improved" and abridged version of the Iliad (1713) changed the account of the death of Hector, "pour rétablir la gloire des deux héros de l'Iliade." In the introductory ode Homer is made to confess that :

> "Mon siècle eut des dieux trop bizarres,
> Des héros d'orgueil infectés,"

and begs La Motte to amend these faults in his translation.[1]

But the attacks of Perrault, Fontenelle, and La Motte are mild and reasonable in comparison with the deliberate vilification of the characters of the great heroes in which Bayle indulged in his Dictionary. He was not content with censuring their ways and actions

[1] Fontenelle in his *Remarques sur le théatre grec* (which Diderot would not accept for the *Encyclopédie* because they were too hostile to the Greeks) wrote : "La description d'Hercule faisant bonne chère, dans *Alceste*, est si burlesque qu'on dirait d'un crocheteur qui est de confrérie" (Rigault, *op. cit.*, p. 163). The same opinion expressed by Wieland in the *Briefe über die Alceste* (1773) roused Goethe to fury and spurred him to write *Götter, Helden und Wieland.* Fontenelle also censured Theocritus for making his shepherds use language "qui répond trop bien à la grossièreté du village" (*Discours sur la nature de l'eglogue*, 1688. See Rigault, p. 164).

as they are generally known from Homer, and the stock of well-known myths; he sought out the obscurest and least authenticated stories, provided only that they were sufficiently discreditable, and enlarged on them with all the skill of his suggestive wit. Achilles is the chief victim of this dishonourable usage. Having, for instance, recounted the rape of Deïdameia, daughter of his host, by Achilles at the age of ten, Bayle continues:[1] "Il ne tarda pas longtemps à traiter de la même sorte Iphigénie," when she was brought to Aulis to be sacrificed. This extraordinary tale, quite unknown to Euripides or to any of the classical Greeks, is supported by only one reference, to a certain Tzetzem "in Lycophron." Yet, when it suits his purpose, Bayle will take almost excessive precautions in weighing and comparing sources. The same authority alone is quoted for the tale that Achilles, having caught sight of Helen on the walls of Troy, could not sleep for desire of her, and requested Thetis to procure her for him. "Bel emploi pour une mère! Thetis ne laissa pas de l'accepter." The charge of unnatural immorality with Patroclus is, of course, not omitted,[2] and an attempt is made[3] to throw doubt even on Achilles' bravery. Bayle is determined, for some reason, to make Achilles appear in the blackest possible colours. "Au reste, le traîtement de ce cadavre [Hector's], les discours qu' Achille tint à Hector prêt à expirer, la liberté qu'il accorda à qui voulut d'insulter et de frapper ce corps mort, cette âme vénale, qui se laissa enfin persuader, à force de riches présens, de rendre à Priam le corps de son fils, sont des choses si éloignées je ne dirai pas de la vertu héroïque, mais de la générosité la plus commune,

[1] Article on Achilles, Note O. [2] Note P. [3] Note L.

qu'il faut nécessairement juger, ou qu' Homère n'avoit aucune idée de l'Héroisme, ou qu'il n'a eu dessein que de peindre un brutal." [1]

Bayle's attacks on Homer and Greek mythology probably had more effect than those of all the other Moderns put together. It is needless here to stress the colossal influence of his Dictionary on all branches of thought in every land throughout the eighteenth century. In Germany it was translated by Gottsched and published at Leipzig in 1741, while Frederick the Great caused an *Extrait du Dictionnaire de Bayle* to be published in Berlin in 1765. It was the universally accepted book of reference on all subjects,[2] and became, as Montgomery says, "the treasury of all 'enlightened' writers in Germany as in France during the first half of the eighteenth century, and in some quarters even longer." Neither Winckelmann nor Lessing was able to escape its spell; and, if it is evident that both had judgment and sense enough to treat Bayle's view of the Greeks with the contempt it deserved, smaller men, with less perspicacity and less knowledge, must have been misled in numbers. Loën's example alone is sufficient proof of Bayle's influence on men of no more than average intelligence. His delight in repeating little-known stories, provided only that they are unsavoury enough, is taken straight from Bayle, and Loën gives the same uncharitable twist to Achilles' motives in the great scene with Priam that is given to them by Bayle in the passage quoted above. Moreover, as Montgomery points out,

[1] Note H.

[2] In the preface to the translation of Anacreon, published by Uz and Götz in 1746, the authors excuse themselves for not having given a life of Anacreon on the ground that it would be "mühsam, einen ganzen Artikel aus Baylens Wörterbuch abzuschreiben."

the Dictionary produced innumerable imitations in Germany, *Konversationslexika* and *Realwörterbücher*, of which Zedler's *Universallexikon* (Halle, 1732–54) was the greatest.[1] Bayle's spirit, if not his actual words, had been the mental food of all cultivated Germans for fifty years before Goethe began to know the Greeks.

It was not only the manners and morals of the Greeks which offended the Moderns. The critical standards of Versailles were applied also to matters of purely literary taste. It is not surprising that Homer should have seemed ill-constructed, long-winded and irrelevant in style, and Pindar confused and extravagant in diction, for French literature had just succeeded in establishing, by a series of supreme works of creative genius, that ideal of formal economy, clarity and precision, which has been its peculiar glory ever since. Homer's similes in particular, with their fertility of irrelevant detail, aroused the wrath of the critics, who could not see that such details were justified and raised above all Reason's laws by their intrinsic beauty. In his fourth *Parallèle* Perrault amused himself by parodying "ces sortes de comparaisons à longues queues," and in *Le Siècle de Louis le Grand*, he had complained of the length of Homer's speeches. In the third volume of the *Parallèles*[2] he pulls the construction of the Iliad to

[1] Montgomery, *op. cit.*, p. 117 and p. 127, footnote 3. Montgomery quotes from the articles on Homer and Achilles; from the former: "Wenn man also dieses Dichters Beschreibungen gegen unsere heutige Sitten und Lebens-Art, oder auch wohl gegen die gesunde Vernunft [= le bon sens], halten will, muss man an ihn nothwendig echt viel auszusetzen finden." And Achilles "wusste sich in der Liebe nicht zu mässigen"; which is mild and general in comparison with Bayle's malicious wealth of detail. But without Bayle it is unlikely that Zedler would have made this reproach at all, for from the story of Achilles as it was then generally known (from Pomey let us say) it was not possible to make the accusation of unusual lustfulness.

[2] P. 40 ff.

pieces, so as to show that all the central part of the poem has nothing whatever to do with the wrath of Achilles, and concludes that it is impossible to see what was Homer's object in writing the Iliad.

One of La Motte's chief reasons for translating Homer was to "improve" him by cutting out all unnecessary matter; which he did with such success that the new Iliad consisted of twelve books instead of twenty-four.

It is not surprising that Pindar found little favour with the Perraults and La Mottes. He is treated in the *Parallèles* in a tone of light raillery: "Le plus celèbre de tous les Grecques en ce genre de Poésie c'est Pindare. Il faut croire qu'il est bien sublime, puisque personne n'y peut atteindre, soit pour l'imiter, soit pour l'entendre."[1] And later Perrault speaks of Pindar's "galimatias impénétrable." The Theban poet came to have the reputation, in Germany as well as in France, of delighting in an unseemly extravagance of expression, and in a bombastic or even ecstatic manner quite fatal to all clarity or decency of form. "It seems people imagine Pindar is always in the clouds, always seeing visions and having ecstasies; everything is splendid, dithyrambic, bold." Thus Uz defined the conventional view of Pindar in his day.[2] The word "Pindaric" was used quite naturally as a term of censure. This is curiously illustrated in the Vorbericht to Hagedorn's *Oden und Lieder* (Hamburg, 1747 and 1754). The author praises the French lyric poets in comparison with the Italians, because the latter are "too Pindaric, too full of similes, too ingenious, and too long." La Motte's influence in this

[1] Vol. III, p. 160.
[2] See Feuerbach, *Uz und Cronegk*, Leipzig, 1866, p. 84.

matter is betrayed by a quotation from the Frenchman's *Discours sur l'Ode*, censuring Horace's and Pindar's lack of form.[1] The Tragedians are lightly dismissed in the *Parallèles* as inferior to Corneille, because they have no love-interest and are therefore boring.[2] And Fontenelle in his *Remarques sur le théâtre grec* calls Aeschylus " une manière de fou " which was remarkably strong language for the man who, even at Versailles, was famous for being utterly incapable of passion.

The Greeks fell short of the Versailles standards not only in manners and in literary form ; they gave offence in a third way : by their irrationality. From the first the crux was the Shield of Achilles. Desmarets, the slightly mad author of Clovis, favourite butt of Boileau's satires, from whom Perrault took most of his ideas,[3] spoke of " des absurdités impossibles, par exemple des figures qui se meuvent et parlent sur un bouclier," [4] and Perrault in *Le Siècle de Louis le Grand* wrote :

> " Ce fameux bouclier, dans un siècle plus sage,
> Eût été plus correct et moins chargé d'ouvrage."

It did not occur to him that, when writing poetry, it is best not to be too " sage." The description of the Shield in the Iliad was one of the passages which La Motte was most proud of having " improved." " Le bouclier d'Achille m'a paru défectueux par plus d'un endroit : j'ai donc imaginé un bouclier qui n'eût point ces défauts." [5] Terrasson continued the attack with all the thoroughness of a trained geometer in his *Dissertation sur l'Iliade* (1715).

[1] Vorbericht, p. 6, note. [2] Dialogue IV, and see Rigault, p. 201.
[3] Rigault, p. 206. [4] Rigault, p. 110.
[5] Preface to translation of Iliad and Rigault, p. 371.

We have seen that Boivin, in *L'Apologie d'Homère*, 1715, tried to reconcile Homer and his critics by demonstrating how all the scenes which Homer describes could be fitted into the ordinary dimensions of a shield. But the honour of Homer among men was not to be brought back by such means. So long as the mathematical laws of Reason were the usual standards for judging poetry, so long as Fontenelle, La Motte and Terrasson could all publicly and with impunity assert that poetry had no function which could not be performed equally well by prose [1]; so long as phantasy was regarded as a form of idiocy, worthy only of children or of primitive savages: so long was Homer condemned to be misunderstood, despised, reviled, or at best patronisingly excused for faults "inevitable under the circumstances"; so long was true appreciation of the Greek spirit impossible. Its colour, its changefulness, its sudden starts of passion and sudden moods of stillness, its store of infinite variety, its deep inconscient beauty could not penetrate to the hearts of men, so long as they were still encased in the arrogant superiority of "perfectibility by Reason."

Few indeed could escape the coercive force of the Versailles canons of social behaviour and literary taste. Even the greatest champion of the ancients, Boileau-Despréaux himself, was never able to judge his idols by their own standards. As Lanson points out,[2] he always remained too much a child of the seventeenth century, too thoroughly a Modern, to be able to discard Versailles standards in judging Homer. And

[1] Fontenelle in *Réflexions sur la poétique*, 1688; La Motte in *Observations sur l'ode de M. de la Faye*; and Terrasson in *Dissertation sur l'Iliade*.

[2] *Histoire de la littérature française*, p. 599.

so he was reduced at times to making rather lame excuses for him. His great reply to Perrault's *Parallèles*, the *Réflexions critiques sur Longin* (1694), did not venture on a general defence or appreciation of Homer, but confined itself to refutation point by point of Perrault's criticisms of detail. The limitation of Boileau's point of view is well illustrated by his treatment of the question of *mots bas*. Perrault had, of course, objected to Homer's use of such words as "ass" and "swineherd." Boileau could not deny the whole doctrine of *mots bas* and proudly assert the right of genius to use what words it likes, "ennobling" them in the act. He grants that "il n'y a rien qui avilisse davantage un discours que les mots bas. On souffrira plutôt une pensée basse exprimée en termes nobles, que la pensée la plus noble exprimées en termes bas." [1] But, he says, among the Greeks "ass" was not a *mot bas*, and so Homer cannot be blamed for using it.[2]

Boileau's subjection to the ideas of his time is of particular importance, for his attitude was essentially reproduced by Gottsched, and thus handed on with fresh authority to German letters. But this distinction must not be forgotten: Boileau admired and loved the Greek writers from intimate knowledge of the original poems, however curiously unsound the reasons for his admiration may sometimes have been; Gottsched, in recommending the ancients as models, merely repeated Boileau's unsound reasons, without

[1] Reflexion IX.

[2] It is of interest to notice that Racine realised the falsity of this attitude and wrote to Boileau to ask him to alter it. Racine was the only Frenchman at this time, besides Fénelon, to appreciate Homer for his deepest qualities of simplicity and naturalness. See Rigault, *op. cit.*, pp. 252 and 253.

being able to impart to his words the conviction of a genuine admiration. For he hardly knew the writers whom he was recommending.

It seems ungracious to criticise the grounds for Boileau's attachment to the ancients, for the fact of that attachment can never be in doubt. Perrault, in his own *mémoires*, has left a description of the scene in the Académie when he read his first attack on the ancients in *Le Siècle de Louis le Grand.* Boileau "s'agitait sur son fauteuil, d'un air d'impatience et de mauvaise humeur . . . grondait tout bas, pendant que Huet, qui siégeait à côté de lui, s'efforçait de le calmer." At last, unable to contain himself any longer, "il se leva avant la fin du discours, en s'écriant qu'une telle lecture était une honte pour l'Académie." [1] And he continued the struggle on behalf of the ancients in the Académie for many years in the face of a hostile majority.

In the later stage of the Quarrel, which broke out in 1713, with La Motte's "improved" translation of the Iliad, the public champion of the ancients was Mme. Dacier, who in 1699 had given to the world the only conscientious and readable version of Homer. Apart from this service to the Humanist cause (whose value can hardly be over-estimated), her efforts on behalf of the ancients were not very successful, and the influence of her critical writings in the later revival of Hellenism is probably not great. In her *Causes de la corruption du goût* (1714), in which she replied to La Motte's attack on Homer, she alienated the sympathy of cultivated society by the violence and unchivalrous directness of her language.

[1] *Mémoires de Charles Perrault,* IV, p. 20, and see Rigault, *op. cit.,* pp. 146 and 147.

The Académie remained generally cool towards the ancients; the younger generation was especially contemptuous; the journals were also hostile; and Homer became the butt even of the popular stage, as in Fuzelier's *Arlequin défenseur d'Homère* and other works.[1]

In Germany, hostility to the ancients was probably never so open as in France. The question never came to a head in a public "quarrel," and so the "modern" attitude never became a clearly formulated doctrine. But such works as Loën's mythology give clear proof of the widespread acceptance of the views of the French Moderns in Germany. Certain of these views received, moreover, the authoritative sanction of Gottsched's name. For though he repeated Boileau's general admonition to imitate the ancient models, he was too typical a product of German Cartesianism to be able to appreciate Greek beauty. It is plain that he admired Homer really only because he won the "respect and admiration" of Aristotle.[2] He refers cautiously to the Quarrel in France, saying that some have "blamed Homer without cause." But in Chapter VI, Part I, he himself rebukes Homer sharply, for offending against "vraisemblance" in the description of the Shield of Achilles. All the objections with which we are familiar from Desmarets, Perrault and Terrasson reappear, and Gottsched concludes: "In short, Homer made a mistake and did not properly observe the probabilities."

Gottsched helped to maintain the ancients in that position of distant reverence, which they had never lost in Germany, as the necessary models for anyone

[1] See Rigault, *op. cit.*, p. 426 foll.
[2] *Critische Dichtkunst.* Third ed., 1742, Part II, Ch. IX, p. 673.

who wished to attempt the intricate branch of applied mathematics known as Poetry. But he did nothing to help on true appreciation of the Greeks. That could not come until his manner of honouring them had been swept away.

In the 'thirties, 'forties and 'fifties of the eighteenth century there was still practically no independent German literary opinion or taste. Germany thought then what France had thought fifty years before. It is for that reason that the Quarrel of the Ancients and Moderns, although in France it was already somewhat ancient history, is of such importance in a study of Humanism in Germany at the time of Goethe's childhood. Only two years before the publication of Winckelmann's *Gedanken über die Nachahmung der Griechen*, the ideas of Perrault, Bayle, and La Motte were still flourishing in certain sections of German society. And it is natural to suppose that they continued to be held for many years after Winckelmann had definitely started the movement in the opposite direction. They cannot have influenced the younger generation positively, but the reaction from them is plainly visible in the views of Herder and the young Goethe. If the Versailles critics had not been so absurdly shocked by Homer's simplicity and naturalness, Goethe would never have rushed so violently into the other extreme when the true Homer was first revealed to him by Herder. The attitude to the Greeks expressed in *Götter, Helden und Wieland*, and implied throughout "Werther," is of course only a symptom of the general repudiation of the social and moral standards of Versailles. But it was a symptom evoked by the corresponding symptom in the previous age. The one cannot be understood without the other.

It is impossible to tell what subtly distorting effects the ideas of the older generation may not have had on the views of the child and the youth, however much he may consciously have repudiated them. We can only say here, as in the matter of actual knowledge of the Greeks, that the " atmosphere " in which Goethe grew up cannot have been good for the formation of a sound basis of ideas on which later to build a balanced and well-proportioned structure.

B. *The Revival.*

(1) *The Gottschedian Halfway House.*

Loën's attitude to the Greeks may have been common enough among the older generation in Goethe's youth, but it was a survival from an earlier age, and was doomed soon to yield to tendencies which had been growing in Germany for twenty years or more. For this revival of general appreciation of the Greeks it is even harder to define a starting-point than for the revival of classical learning. We may say that both started at about the same time—between 1730 and 1740. Gottsched's influence, despite the great limitations of his attitude to Greek literature, was certainly generally favourable to a renewed interest in the Classics. In the preface to the collection of works by Lucian, which he edited in 1745, he wrote: "I might perhaps without boastfulness assert that I am one of those who have once again made known the true beauties of ancient poetry and eloquence after they had been obscured by many neo-French rules and examples of a quite peculiar poetic art borrowed from Lohenstein and Hoffmannswaldau."[1] Though a certain amount must be discounted for Gottsched's vanity, it remains true that the Baroque provided an atmosphere most uncongenial to the Greek spirit and that the new ideals introduced by Gottsched allowed in some ways of a more appreciative attitude, although, of course, the fundamental Rationalism of Gottsched's classicism made a true appreciation impossible. Montgomery gives Gottsched the

[1] *Lucians auserlesene Schriften durch verschiedene Feder verdeutscht,* Leipzig, 1745, Vorrede.

credit of having served the humanist revival by arousing interest in the works of the Daciers and Boileau.[1] He did, in fact, attract the serious attention of the cultivated world back to the ancients, if only by definitely recommending them as models, as Boileau had done, although he did little to teach the public how to direct its attention to the proper points.

The extent to which interest in the Greeks had grown by the middle of the century is curiously proved by an essay which Hagedorn published in the same volume with his *Oden und Lieder* (1747). The subject of the essay, which is very long, is the skolia or drinking-songs of the ancient Greeks. In a quasi-learned style of great dryness, Hagedorn gives an account of the different types of skolion, with the minutest details of the manner in which they were sung. For four pages he discusses the thrilling question of whether the myrtle twig which the singer held was passed round from neighbour to neighbour, or backwards and forwards across the table. He produces a terrifying show of authorities and sources. In support of one assertion he quotes Favorinus, Athenæus, Pollux, Hesychius, the Scholiast of Aristophanes, Suidas, Eustathius, and the compiler of the Etymologicon. Whether Hagedorn had really read all or any of these may be doubted. But that is not the point. The extraordinary thing is that Hagedorn should have thought fit to append this essay, which is intensely dull, to a collection of light and trivial verses intended merely to amuse and delight those ladies of Hamburg society who affected a taste for literature. It seems necessary to suppose that in 1747

[1] Montgomery, *op. cit.*, p. 144.

there was already some sort of fashion in Greek things which made such an essay tolerable. It is a tiny indication from which too much must not be deduced; but it is significant of the way in which things were moving in the great world.

Gottsched's admonition to German authors to return to the ancient forms could be followed with success only in one branch of literature. The German muse was not strong enough to attempt the larger forms even with the support of ancient models, but the imitation of Greek lyric as "Anacreon" had written it was not beyond her powers. The Anacreontic vogue of the 'forties and 'fifties represents the literary expression of the Gottschedian attitude to the Greeks. The poets of the Anacreontic school were all, more or less, actively opposed to Gottsched on the general questions of the *Literaturstreit*, which was then at its height, but on the question of the use or abuse of Greek literature they followed Gottsched unquestioningly. Their chief object was merely to give the German language greater lightness, grace and flexibility and to impose on the German lyric the compression and simplicity of form which it lacked. For this purpose the closest possible imitation, which amounted, in fact, if not in name, to translation, was necessary. The *Oden Anakreons*, published in 1746 by Uz and Götz, were frankly called translations. Gleim's Anacreontics, which had appeared in the previous year, were entitled merely *Scherzhafte Lieder*, and contained alterations and additions, which called down a rebuke from Uz. "Your manner of translating is more a paraphrase, and has additions, which are very pretty but are not in accordance with the simplicity of the old Greek, who expresses himself shortly and without any unnecessary words."[1] Gleim himself seems to have accepted this view later. In 1757 he was revising his *Scherzhafte Lieder*, and wrote to Kleist (Oct. 17, 1757) that he was horrified to find "so little that is perfect in the spirit of Anacreon."

The imitation of the Greek model was not confined to the form. In the preface to the translation he made with Uz, Götz wrote : "As far as this translation is concerned I can assure you that it has been made in Anacreon's spirit (Sinn) ; that is according to his feelings (Empfindungen) as well as according to his manner of expression." Gleim went so far as to claim for his *Lieder nach dem Anakreon* (1763), that they would reveal to German eyes "the prettiest pictures and the most delicate feelings of the Greeks."

By 1763 it was becoming the fashion to talk with a fine vagueness of "the Greek spirit." But in the 'forties, the years of the true Anacreontic, the Greeks did not stand for anything so serious as a *Weltanschauung*. They merely provided the models for the different literary genres. Since the model for lyric poetry had sung of a carefree life of flirtations and wine, his imitators must do the same and try to infuse into their own poems something of the Teian's eternal cheerfulness. This was all that imitation of the Greek spirit amounted to with Uz, Gleim and Götz, and with Hagedorn too, who differed from the three Anacreontic poets only by his freer imitation of the form. Unfortunately, when people began to be interested in Hellenism for its own sake, they naturally attributed to the Greeks as a whole the philosophy and the manners which were familiar to them from the German Anacreontic. This question will be discussed

[1] See Feuerbach, *Uz und Cronegk*, Leipzig, 1866, p. 40.

later. For the moment it is only important to realise that the Anacreontic was merely the expression of the Gottschedian attitude to the Greeks. It used them as models, without concerning itself about the *Weltanschauung* which the forms expressed. Indeed Gleim and Uz prided themselves on the fact that they had never lived the life which they sang in their poems. "I sing of wine and of love, yet have as little experience of the one as of the other." [1] And Gleim wrote to Kleist: "We who were wont to sing of wine and love, but drank and loved very little." [2] Gleim was only once in love with a woman—not very seriously; and Körte describes a carouse *à l'Anacréontique* in which Gleim and Klopstock took part. Crowned with roses, whose fragrance aroused in them "Anakreontische Lust," they kept it up all night till the sun rose. But the second bottle was left unfinished at this refined symposium.

(2) *The Approach to True Hellenism.*

Gottsched and the Anacreontiker were putting the cart before the horse. Before the ancients could serve as models of form, men had to learn to appreciate and love the content of their works, the manner of their thought, the whole of their attitude to art and to life. Winckelmann was the first to become conscious of this, but the process was started in Germany by Breitinger. There is no trace in Breitinger of Winckelmann's reckless glorification of the whole Greek way of life, but the Swiss critic was the first in Germany to appreciate Greek poetry, and especially Homer, for

[1] Letter from Uz to Gleim. See Feuerbach, *op. cit.*, p. 32.
[2] See Körte's *Leben Gleims*, Halberstadt, 1811, p. 86.

those qualities in which it really excels. His *Critische Abhandlung von der Natur, den Absichten und dem Gebrauch der Gleichnisse*, published at Zürich in 1740, was one of the earliest signs of the break-up of the rationalistic standards of criticism, which had done so much harm to Greek literature.[1] There is still a great deal of talk of "rules," and, though the phantasy is allowed a more important place in the poet's outfit than ever Gottsched would give it, such phrases as "die Logik der Phantasie" show how completely the bogey of rationalism still ruled the Swiss critic's theory. Nevertheless, in practice, Breitinger shows a real appreciation of the irrational essence of poetry.

Throughout the essay Homer is quoted with approval and admiration to illustrate the different uses of the simile in poetry. Breitinger did for Homer precisely what Gottsched could not do. He supported his injunction to imitate Homer with reasons and examples drawn from a loving acquaintance with the Iliad and the Odyssey. His enthusiasm carried conviction, while Gottsched's frigidly dutiful recommendation passed unheeded. Breitinger openly attacked La Motte and Perrault for their criticism of Homer's use of similes. In the fifth chapter he defends the "comparaisons à longue queue" which had aroused Perrault's mockery. Breitinger admits that Homer's similes are often irrelevant. "The likeness does not continue for more than a line or two, but the poet carries the idea further, until he develops out of it a fine thought, which is calculated to fire the reader's mind and to achieve that lofty form of

[1] See Montgomery, *op. cit.*, p. 146. But as Schneider (*Zwischen Barock und Klassizismus*, p. 74) points out, it was only the first step, and not at all a revolutionary one. See also p. 78 for the Swiss treatment of *Phantasie*.

pleasure which accords with the nature of an heroic poem."[1] Even this defence sounds a little prosaic and solemn, but there are moments when the stolid Switzer forgets himself altogether in the enchantment of pure poetry. As an example of the simile which deliberately goes beyond the strict points of comparison in order to create beautiful images, he quotes the famous passage in Iliad VIII, where the camp fires of the Greeks are compared to the stars shining on a windless night over the mountains and glades, "and the shepherd joyeth in his heart." With a delightful spontaneity Breitinger bursts out: "This simile changes the earth at a stroke into a starry heaven."

It was this capacity to be carried away by the magic of words, not by their sense, which was to make possible the revival of Hellenism. Breitinger was the first Teuton to show it, and openly to teach its value. "The stranger Homeric similes appear," he writes, "the more artistic and effective are they in general, if viewed in the right light."[2] This was the lie direct to the Perraults and La Mottes, and the first hint of the coming Herders.

Presumably the new attitude to Homer spread slowly through the public in the fifteen years following the publication of Breitinger's essay. In Germany no critic thought it worth while to reassert or develop it. But the whole trend of thought in these years favoured its gradual acceptance, and the instant response of the public to the uncompromising Hellenism of Winckelmann's *Gedanken über die Nachahmung*

[1] *Critische Abhandlung von der Natur, den Absichten und dem Gebrauch der Gleichnisse*, Zürich, 1740, Abschnitt 5, p. 142.
[2] Abschnitt 12, p. 374.

der Griechen in der Malerei und Bildhauerkunst,[1] proves how much greater a change had taken place than ever Breitinger had contemplated.

I cannot deal with the æsthetic ideas which Winckelmann's *Gedanken* put forward, nor with their influence on later German Hellenism. I wish only to discuss Winckelmann's attitude to the Greeks as a whole and to make it clear what an unbelievable advance it represents on that of his time. The *Gedanken* were lightning out of a clear sky. It was not merely that in them the imitation of the ancients was recommended with a fire of passionate conviction which was utterly lacking with Gottsched.[2] Winckelmann held up the Greeks to the admiration of his fellow countrymen in their manner of life as well as in their art, and indeed derived the perfection of their art from the excellence of their life. This idea of Winckelmann's is the seed of the whole of German Classicism, which continued, as it developed with Goethe and Schiller, to stress more and more the way of life of the Greeks, and to regard their art merely as the expression of this way of life. "The explanation of the beauty of Greek art lies in the beauty of the Greek man." [3] Winckelmann does not state this conviction in so many words, but it is implicit in all the first part of the essay. The Greek artists had unrivalled opportunities for studying beauty in the world around them ; in particular they had the gymnasia where they could observe the human body in free and natural action. And what human bodies ! The fairest there have ever been. "The fairest body amongst

[1] Published in Dresden, 1755.

[2] "Der einzige Weg für uns, gross, ja, wenn es möglich ist, unnachahmlich zu werden, ist die Nachahmung der Alten."

[3] Korff, *Geist der Goethezeit*, Vol. II, p. 309.

us would perhaps not approach the fairest Greek body more nearly than did Iphides approach his brother Hercules." The reason for this beauty was the free, healthy, vigorous life which the Greek youth led. "Take a young Spartan born of a hero and heroine, never cramped in babyhood by swaddling clothes, and accustomed from his seventh year to sleep on the ground and to practise wrestling and swimming. Compare him with a young sybarite of our own day and then judge which of the two the artist would choose as his model for a young Theseus, an Achilles, or even a Bacchus." [1] The Greek dress was designed, unlike "our cramping and compressing clothing of to-day," to leave the body free to grow as Nature wished. Beauty of form was publicly encouraged by "Wett-Spiele der Schönheit." Disfiguring diseases were unknown in Greece. The tone implies that even this fortunate dispensation was in some way due to the excellence of the Greek mode of life. He sums up: "In short, everything that had been taught and impressed upon them through nature and art from birth to manhood about the training of the body, and the perfecting and adornment of that training, was used to promote the natural beauty of the ancient Greeks. That the beauty of their bodies was far in advance of ours may be asserted with the greatest probability."

But the Greeks had not merely bodily beauty. The nobility of feeling of their art would have been impossible if they had not been spiritually as beautiful as in their bodies. "The prologue to many of the Dialogues of Plato, which he represents as arising in the gymnasia of Athens, give us a picture of the noble

[1] Observe how much—perhaps unconsciously—there is of Rousseau in this passage.

souls of these youths." The Greeks were in every way "the most perfect creations of nature," for "in Greece, where man could devote himself to joy and delight from his youth up, and where the bourgeois respectability of to-day never interfered with the freedom of manners, natural beauty could show itself undisguised to the great advantage of the artists." This is really the most significant sentence in the whole essay, though it probably passed unnoticed at the time of publication. It held the seed of Goethe's attitude to morality in his classical period, the ideal of the naturally moral man, who is above the constraints of the laws of conventional morality, who possesses the restraining forces in his own character, and can therefore, without fear, love and enjoy life as an absolute good.[1] But this ideal was always too high and difficult for most of mankind, and certainly, in 1755, the general public was in no position to be influenced by Winckelmann's hint. It was enough if they could be induced to catch some of the fire of admiration which burned in Winckelmann's words for the more obvious beauties of the Greek life.

But the real theme of the essay is Greek art. The praise of the Greek way of life does not cover every aspect of that life, but only such as affected the achievements of the artists. Greek art is, however, systematically, if broadly, surveyed, and in every field Winckelmann finds superiority over the art of his own day. The absolute rightness of the contour in Greek sculpture, neither too thin nor too fleshy; the supreme command of drapery; above all the majestic restraint in expression, the "noble simplicity and silent strength" in comparison with the "fiery boldness,"

[1] See Korff, Vol. II, p. 287 foll.

the "*Franchezza*," as they call it, of Baroque sculpture and painting—these were the primary advantages of the Greeks over the moderns. Even in matters of technique we can learn a lesson from the Greeks: for several pages he discusses methods of modelling and casting, and concludes that the Greeks knew best; so that even Perrault's claim that the moderns are necessarily superior in the mechanics of art cannot stand examination.

Winckelmann went further than merely to prove that the Greeks were better than the moderns; he held them up as the absolute ideal in art, the ideal whose imitation would lead more quickly to the creation of beauty than direct imitation of nature. The Greeks were not content merely to copy nature (a nature already more beautiful than ours) but added something to nature, an ideal beauty, which is never found in any of the separate parts of nature. "Those who know and imitate Greek works find in these masterpieces not only nature at its best, but something more than nature; that is certain ideal beauties formed from pictures created only in the mind of the artist." Therefore, the surest, simplest, quickest way to create new beauty in art is to give up working from nature and to work only from the antique. "Does it not follow from this that the beauty of Greek sculpture is more easily apprehended than the beauty of nature, and that the former is therefore more concentrated and less dispersed in its appeal than the latter? Hence the study of nature must at any rate be a longer and more toilsome road to the knowledge of perfect beauty than the study of the antique."

Here is the crowning effrontery of this divinely-inspired work. Little wonder that Gottsched was shocked by the excessive praise of the Greeks in the essay as a whole, and that the experts, connoisseurs and archæologists alike, condemned it.[1] It treated far too cavalierly all the difficulties and intricacies of their profession. But in the cultivated public its success was immediate, great and lasting. Winckelmann became famous in a night; and more—he at once attained the position of being the recognised authority on his subject. When he went to Italy, all eyes followed him and awaited expectantly the first fruits of his researches there.[2] The general public had in fact for some time been in advance of its nominal leaders in the matter of appreciation of Greek art and the Greek spirit. There was a great deal of vaguely pro-Hellenic feeling which was only waiting for a clear lead. The *Gedanken* gave this lead and thus started the German Neo-Hellenic movement.

But no pioneer in a new movement of thought or taste works entirely without assistance from earlier men. Winckelmann found the ground prepared, the public favourably disposed, so that the seed he sowed took root and flourished. I have already mentioned Breitinger's part in the awakening of public enthusiasm for the Greeks. He was the only German forerunner of Winckelmann, and even he had many of his ideas from abroad.[3] Again we must turn to France, and as before to the France of an earlier generation, to find the source of that stream of ideas which first moistened the soil around the desiccated seeds of German humanism.

Despite the general antipathy to the ancients in

[1] Justi, p. 434 foll. [2] *Ibid.*, p. 382.
[3] See Montgomery, *op. cit.*, p. 148.

French society at the end of the seventeenth century, there were some great spirits who could see through the prejudices of their time to the beauty that dwelt on the shores of the Ægean in the youth of the world. Racine's poetic soul was open to its influence. But it was Fénelon whose task it was to pass on his love of antiquity to generations more ready to listen than his own.

I might have dealt with Fénelon in discussing the Quarrel of the Ancients and Moderns, for, with Mme. Dacier, he was the champion of the ancients during the second stage of the quarrel, although it is true he never appeared openly to take a side. But it has been preferable to postpone an account of his ideas until this point, because so many of them became the basis for the revival of Hellenism in Germany with which we are now concerned. One may often trace a direct line of descent from Fénelon to Herder and so to Goethe. In this he differs from Boileau, whose influence was mostly sterile and died out in the Gottschedian wastes.

Fénelon's admiration for the ancients was founded on a thorough and loving acquaintance with their works. He would have satisfied perfectly Macaulay's definition of a scholar as one who can read Plato with his feet on the fender.[1] And it was far more than a literary admiration. It was, as Rigault says, an " idée morale." The ancients represented certain human qualities and virtues, which could not be found in the contemporary world.

For this reason his defence of ancient literature has a glow of sincerity and conviction which must have made it peculiarly hard to resist. He was only once

[1] See Montgomery, *op. cit.*, p. 132, note 3.

drawn into making a set comparison of the ancients and the moderns, in the *Lettre sur les occupations de l'académie*, which he wrote in 1714 at the request of Mme. Dacier. Despite an appearance of impartiality and fair-mindedness Fénelon's verdict falls unequivocally on the side of the ancients. The mere authority of his opinion must have done much to break down the prejudice against the ancients which had grown to such an absurd pitch in the early eighteenth century.

But of far more interest to us are those passages in the *Lettre à l'académie* which betray the basis of Fénelon's moral admiration of the Greeks. His unique importance lies in the fact that he admired and loved Greek civilisation precisely because of those characteristics which disgusted his contemporaries. It was the simplicity, the frugality and the directness of the Homeric age which attracted him, and the reflexion of these qualities in its poetry made Homer the king of poets in his eyes. "Cette simplicité de mœurs semble ramener l'âge d'or. Le bon homme Eumée me touche bien plus qu'un héros de Clélie ou de Cleopâtre. Les vains préjugés de notre temps avilissent de telles beautés : mais nos défauts ne diminuent point la vrai prix d'une vie si raisonnable et si naturelle. Malheur à ceux qui ne sentent point le charme de ces vers"![1] Here is a frontal attack on the whole Versailles school of criticism, as well as on Versailles itself! "Diverses personnes sont dégoûtées de la frugalité des mœurs qu'Homère dépeint. Mais . . . rien n'est si aimable que cette vie des premiers hommes."[2] "Homère n'a-t-il pas dépeint avec

[1] *Lettre à l'académie, Fénelon Œuvres*, Anonymous edition, *Imprimerie du roi*, 1820, Vol. XXI, p. 199.
[2] P. 252.

grâce l'île de Calypso et les jardins d'Alcinous, sans y mettre ni marbre ni dorure? Les occupations de Nausicaa ne sont elles pas plus estimables que le jeu et que les intrigues des femmes de notre temps." [1] In fact, he concludes, "c'est notre folle et cruelle vanité et non pas la noble simplicité des anciens, qu'il faut corriger."

The *Lettre à l'académie* probably had little effect on the general public either in France or Germany, although there is evidence of its direct influence on Herder. But Fénelon's noble passion for Greek simplicity found expression also in a book which became the daily reading of thousands in Germany.

Les Aventures de Télémaque, published in 1699, did not begin to assert its influence in Germany until 1730, and was most active from 1750 until about 1780.[2] The precise nature of this influence is hard to estimate. Montgomery says: "It appears certain that its author was one of the chief *officiers de liaison* between the eighteenth century and Homer: and Télémaque forms a valuable bridge from the classicism of Gottsched's day to the Hellenism in Goethe's." [3] The limitations of the Hellenism of *Télémaque*—in particular its priggishness and the faint flavour of Versailles which even Fénelon could not entirely exclude from the setting—are so obvious that it is at first hard to see how it can have helped on the revival of true Hellenism. But it was just this subtle compromise which gave it its power. It introduced the Greek heroes to the public under a guise which showed them to be after all not such monsters of barbarism as the Moderns made out. The habit of

[1] *Lettre à l'académie*, p. 253.
[2] See Montgomery, *op. cit.*, pp. 132 and 143. [3] *Ibid.*, p. 132.

admiration once established, it was possible for later readers to peel off the Versailles veneer and discover the true hero beneath. As Montgomery says: "Precisely through its skilful, subconscious mingling of Versailles with the gardens of Alcinous, of Homeric personages with Christian precepts, *Télémaque* enchanted the eighteenth century and helped to prepare the way for the purer Hellenism of its later years." [1]

Nevertheless Fénelon does not always compromise. In some passages his love of Greek simplicity is as clearly expressed as in those already quoted from the *Lettre à l'académie.* One in particular must be quoted in full, because of the extraordinary resemblance between its views and those which Rousseau made general in the last half of the century.

Telemachus, on the routine visit which all epic heroes have to pay to the lower world, is shown the shades of "enlightened despots" of antiquity who thought only of the happiness of their peoples, and who now dwell in the Elysian Fields in the realm of highest bliss. Among these is Triptolemus, who taught the Greeks the science of agriculture. This was the first step away from barbarism. "Les peuples mêmes sauvages et farouches, qui couroient épars, çà et là, dans les forêts d'Epire et d'Étolie pour se nourrir de gland, adoucirent leurs mœurs, et se soumirent à des lois, quand ils eurent appris à faire croître des moissons et à se nourrir de pain. Triptolème fit sentir aux Grecs le plaisir qu'il y a à ne devoir ses richesses qu'à son travail, et à trouver dans son champ tout ce qu'il faut pour rendre la vie

[1] Montgomery, *op. cit.*, p. 135.

commode et heureuse. Cette abondance si simple et si innocente, qui est attachée à l'agriculture, les fit souvenir des sages conseils d'Erichthon. Ils méprisèrent l'argent et toutes les richesses artificielles qui ne sont richesses qu'en imagination, qui tentent les hommes de chercher des plaisirs dangereux, et qui les détournent du travail, où ils trouveroient tous les biens réels, avec des mœurs pures, dans une pleine liberté . . . Heureux les Grecs, s'ils étoient demeurés fermes dans ces maximes, si propres à les rendre puissans, libres, heureux, et dignes de l'être par une solide vertu ! Mais hélas ! ils commencent à admirer les fausses richesses, ils négligent peu à peu les vraies, et ils dégénèrent de cette merveilleuse simplicité." [1]

Here is something different from Boileau's purely æsthetic admiration of the Greeks as literary models. It shows a tendency to idealise Greek civilisation as the youth of the world, the Golden Age of innocent bliss, which, as Montgomery says, " became increasingly harder to resist in the minds of Rousseau, Gessner and Herder . . . and became a conviction in Herder and Schiller," and, one may add, for a time at least in Goethe.

It is true that the Greeks whom Fénelon here praises are those of a most primitive, pre-Homeric age. The fifth-century Athenians, of whom we first think when we speak of the Greeks, could never deserve praise on these grounds. The distinction may have been clear enough to Fénelon, who was a scholar, but it was most certainly not clear to the average reader in the 'fifties and 'sixties of the eighteenth century. The world of difference, of which we are so

[1] *Télémaque*, Book XIV, Ed. cit. Vol. XX, p. 403.

well aware, between Odysseus' Ithaca and the Athens of Pericles, was quite unsuspected by the general public. Probably even to Goethe it was vague enough.

In this description of the contented Greek husbandman Fénelon painted Rousseau's "homme naturel" perhaps more accurately than Jean-Jacques himself was ever prepared to do. Rousseau did not concern himself very much with the Greeks, and his opinion of them varied from moment to moment, but there are passages, particularly in *Émile,* which Fénelon himself could have written. The simple garden of Sophie's father is likened with approval to the Gardens of Alcinous.[1] In a footnote Homer's description is translated and this ironical remark added: "Telle est la description du jardin royal d'Alcinous, au septième livre de l'Odyssée ; jardin dans lequel, à la honte de ce vieux rêveur d'Homêre et des princes de son temps, on ne voit ni treillages, ni statues, ni cascades ni boulingrins." In the same passage Nausicaa is set up as a model to Sophie because she did not disdain to wash the household linen herself. The wheel had come full circle. What seemed, except to Fénelon, a shame and a reproach to Homer and his day, is now held up to general admiration by the prophet of the hour.

In most of the few passages where Rousseau mentions the Greeks he praises them for some custom more in accordance with the natural law than the modern habit. For instance, after marriage Greek women were no longer seen in public : "renfermées dans leurs maisons, elles bornaient tous leurs soins à leur ménage et à leur famille. Celle est la manière

[1] *Émile,* Bk. V.

de vivre que la nature et la raison prescrivent au sexe."[1] And the idea—which Winckelmann perhaps took straight from Rousseau—that the bodily beauty of the Greeks, as we see it in their statues, was due to their easy, healthy clothing, is found in the same book of *Émile*.

In one passage in the *Essai sur l'origine des langues* (Ch. VI) Homer, the divine singer, is praised at the expense of the later writers of "literature." "Les autres poètes écrivoient, Homère seul avait chanté ; et ses chants divins n'ont cessé d'être écoutés avec ravissement que quand l'Europe s'est couverte de barbares, qui se sont mêlés de juger ce qu'ils ne pouvoient sentir." It was this attitude of Rousseau to Homer which prevailed in Germany in the Sturm und Drang period, and not that of the essay *De l'imitation théâtrale*, where Rousseau simply revives Plato's moral objections to poets in general and Homer in particular from the tenth book of the *Republic*. It is just such a piece of frigid argumentation as would have been most distasteful to the spirits of the Geniezeit.[2]

It is not in these few references that Rousseau did his best work for the Greeks. His whole attack on the conventions, on the over-sophistications of society and on the tyranny of Reason freed men's minds to love once again the richness and the sincerity of the message of Hellas. If he himself never identified the Greeks with his ideal of humanity, other less cautious minds found the resemblance irresistible ; and if he continued to distrust the seductive charm of Greek literature, those disciples who had learnt all too well

[1] *Émile*, Bk. V.
[2] See Montgomery, *op. cit.*, p. 163.

how to open their hearts to every influence of beauty and passion, could not but find in Homer and in Pindar food enough for their strange new longings.[1]

Although Fénelon defended the Greeks against many charges of "grossièreté," he himself could not condone the brutality and violent passions of the heroes of the Iliad. Achilles is an "homme fougueux, plus facile à irriter que la mer la plus orageuse."[2] The gods sent him on earth to punish men for their crimes, but they cut short the tale of his days out of pity for his future subjects. The warrior heroes, Achilles, Agamemnon and Ajax, are not allowed into the realm of perfect bliss in the lower world, but "conservent encore ici leurs peines et leurs défauts." But there is, needless to say, no suggestion of Bayle's malicious and carping tone. Behind the dignified condemnation of their excessive fierceness lurks a deep admiration for the heroes as great and splendid figures of grandeur and beauty. He speaks with a tender sadness of Achilles' death. "Les Parques ont accourci le fil de ses jours ; il a été comme une fleur à peine éclose que le tranchant de la charrue coupe, et qui tombe avant la fin du jour où l'on l'avoit vu naître."

[1] Voltaire's attitude to the Greeks is not without interest. It represents the genuine but unstampeded admiration of the late Aufklärung. Justi, with typical German prejudice against Voltaire, twists the emphasis so as to give precisely the false impression (see the *Life of Winckelmann*, Vol. I, p. 147). In the *Essai sur la poesie épique* Voltaire admits a number of faults in Homer but declares that his beauties far excel his faults. He sees Homer's chief merit in having been "un peintre sublime," and admires his similes unreservedly. One may laugh at Patroclus for cooking dinner for Achilles and himself: "Achille et Patrocle n'en sont pas moins éclatants." "La Motte a ôté beaucoup de défauts à Homère, mais il n'a conservé aucune de ses beautés." See also *Siècle de Louis XIV*, Ecrivains Français : Perrault and Mme. Dacier.

[2] *Télémaque*, Book XIV, Ed. cit. Vol. XX, p. 398.

The treatment of the heroes in *Télémaque* must have helped powerfully to reinstate them in the position of honour which they had lost at the beginning of the eighteenth century. It is a far cry from Fénelon's reluctant admiration to the reckless glorification of virtues and faults alike which we find in *Götter, Helden und Wieland.* But there are intermediate steps which indicate the direct line of development from the seventeenth century moralist to the young Titan of the Geniezeit.

Batteaux for instance, who did so much to restore the Greeks to favour in the middle of the century,[1] realised clearly not merely the dominating importance of Achilles' character in the Iliad, but the supreme beauty and greatness of that character when judged simply by human standards. In his *Principes de la Littérature* (1747–50) he wrote: "Achille possède dans un degré éminent la force d'Ajax, la valeur de Diomède, le courage d'Ulysse. Les autres caractères, quelques brillants qu'ils soient, ne sont que des ombres auprès de lui: tout lui cède: rien n'ose lui résister. Il a des sentiments généreux pour Patrocle: il est ami tendre, zélé: il aime les peuples; et quoiqu' excessivement colère et violent, il se retient et respecte les dieux, Priam, même Agamemnon."[2] As Montgomery says, this attitude of generous appreciation towards the Greek heroes was an anticipation of Herder by thirty-six years.

Montgomery also quotes from an essay by the French Hellenist Chabanon, entitled *Dissertation sur Homère considéré comme poète tragique*, published in 1760 and translated into German in 1767. Achilles'

[1] See Montgomery, *op. cit.*, pp. 152–157.
[2] *Ibid.*, p. 155.

tendency to excessive rage is defended as being a trait of greatness proper in the mighty hero of a great poem. He is always great and splendid: "he always retains the mien of greatness . . . he defends the righteous cause with the enthusiasm of passion." His indignation at the wrong done to him by Agamemnon is just and noble. Cold moralists may blame "the criminal transgressions of the Homeric hero"; they only prove themselves to be incapable of feeling.[1]

By the time Goethe went to Leipzig the Greek heroes were losing their bad reputation, and taking on the glamour of distant and romantic figures, symbols of strength and goodness, shining from a world of ideal simplicity and truth. No doubt the view of Bayle and Loën was still powerful, but its very persistence probably drove the younger generation into a more exaggerated attitude of admiration. At any rate the "atmosphere" on this matter as on all others must have been just in a critical state of uncertainty and change. There can have been no solid basis of proven and accepted ideas, such as we possess and hardly notice to-day, and anyone who had to make up his mind what he thought of Achilles' treatment of Hector, had to go very warily if he would not fall into exaggeration on one side or the other.

While Goethe was at Leipzig, a book appeared in which all those tendencies came to expression that had been growing and gathering throughout the century since the publication of *Télémaque*. In 1768 a Swiss named Iselin brought out a *History of Mankind*, in two volumes, in which the Greeks naturally

[1] See Montgomery, *op. cit.*, pp. 173 and 174.

occupied an important place.[1] In the following passage Winckelmann himself might be speaking: "The Greeks seem to have been chosen out by the exceptional favour of Nature to combine all talents and virtues that make nations brilliant, and to be an object of wonderment, an example and model, and the nursery of freedom, learning and art for all following generations." [2] Iselin's view of the heroes is a development of that of Batteaux and Chabanon: "So arose heroes, who answered no call but the lofty feelings of nobility and charity, and dedicated their whole lives and all their powers to the protection of innocence and the maintenance of justice." [3] One pictures Sir Achilles, with his squire Patroclus, pricking o'er the plain to the rescue of distressed damsels. It is a good example of the lengths to which ignorant idealisation could go in these years.

The early republics were, according to Iselin, pools of simple-hearted contentment à la Rousseau. "Thus the stage was set for the development of civic virtue and honour. . . . The posts of honour rarely fell to others than worthy or seemingly worthy men. It was practically impossible that an incompetent person should have endeavoured to attain to them." [4] Happy Iselin, that his desire to idealise the Greek republics was not thwarted by a knowledge of the real conditions!

Sparta receives special praise for the permanence of its institutions and of the true republican virtue. In other states the early happy condition soon passed,

[1] Wieland seems to have used it for his lectures at Erfurt. (See Schaumkell, *Herder als Kulturhistoriker*, 1901, who quotes Wegeler, *Gesch. der d. Historiographie*, 1885.)
[2] Bk. VII, Vol. II, p. 140.
[3] P. 144.
[4] Pp. 172 and 176.

and most sank into " the most unbridled and detestable democracy." But these had the compensation of their arts, which grew to greater and greater perfection as prosperity increased.[1] The feeling for beauty lasted long after all their moral virtues had gone.

Written by a man of no particular distinction, Iselin's *Geschichte der Menschheit* reflects with as much accuracy as we could hope to find the attitude of the general public to the Greeks, just at the time when Goethe was beginning to take a serious interest in Hellenic culture. It shows for the most part an enthusiasm founded on no accurate knowledge and a tendency to sweeping generalisations, whether favourable or unfavourable, which marks an attempt to see the problem as a whole, but which reveals very clearly the lack of a settled background of accepted truths.

[1] P. 192 ff.

C. *The Greeks in Rococo Literature.*

The effect of the new French criticism from Fénelon to Le Bossu and Rousseau was rather destructive of the old hostility to the Greeks than constructive of any clear picture of them. Winckelmann had definite ideas of their qualities, and it was his view which eventually formed the foundation of Goethe's mature classicism. But despite the great success of his *Gedanken über die Nachahmung*, it was natural that his ideas should not be immediately and completely adopted by the cultivated public. For there was a traditional view of the Greeks, which dominated popular thought during Goethe's boyhood and youth, and which was fundamentally incompatible with the new attitude of Fénelon and Winckelmann. Despite this incompatibility the traditional view, which we may call Rococo-Hellenism, did not wane in popularity as the ideas of Fénelon and Le Bossu took firmer hold, but by skilfully adapting some of their ideas and taking advantage of the generally growing interest in the Greeks, established itself for a time as the orthodox view at least among the ignorant public.

The culmination of Rococo-Hellenism appeared in Wieland's work. He reflected the attitude of that part of the public which was most influenced by French fashions and tastes, and also, by the seductive skill and charm with which he wrote, strengthened and popularised that attitude. I cannot go into the whole question of Wieland's view of the Greeks, and of his use of Greek material ; it is a subject which deserves a monograph to itself. I shall merely quote some typical passages from his works, in order to show what picture of the Greeks an ordinarily ignorant reader would get from them.

There are many traits in Wieland which are borrowed straight from Rousseau and Winckelmann ; but the core of his doctrine is that traditional view to which the pioneers of the Neo-Hellenism were most bitterly opposed. In Germany the tradition came down from Gottsched through the Anacreontic poets, Hagedorn, Gleim, Uz and Götz. The Anakreontiker did not greatly concern themselves whether or not their model represented a truly Greek attitude to life. But the public naturally took their picture as a picture of Greek life, and fitted its conception of Greek art, which was founded on no real knowledge, to that picture.[1] The influence of the Anacreontic in Germany was entirely bad from the point of view of a revival of true Hellenism, for it gave the ignorant a false idea of the Greeks, and provided no compensation in the form of instruction or information, as Wieland did. Köster describes the conception of Greek life which derived from the Anakreontiker as " the idea of an effeminate, shallow gaiety, for which the flirtatious, rose-wreathed old singer, Cythera's darling, set the tone, and which he untiringly praised with winey lips." [2]

Women and wine were the only needs for happiness in this world of roses—pink and white girls with a store of easy kisses on pretty lips, and no deeper feelings than what Bacchus could lend them when the torches

[1] " Ein ganz falsches Bild von griechischem Wesen und griechischer Kunst, das wirkliche Kenner ernstlich verstimmen konnte, setzte sich auf lange Zeit fest " (Köster, *Die d. Lit. der Aufklärungszeit*, Heidelberg, 1925, p. 24).

[2] *Ibid.*

were taken away; a world composed of the vulgarest passions, yet so refined away that no passion, but only the vulgarity, remained; where everything must be "tender," "elegant," "charming," "delicate," and strength or sincerity was unpardonable grossness. No storm-breathing Godhead had ever approached "this trifling, flower-crowned Anacreon."

This was the basis of Wieland's picture of the Greeks,[1] despite copious borrowings and adaptations of ideas from Winckelmann and Rousseau. The only works which are of importance for my purpose are *Die Grazien* (1769), and *Agathon* (1766). *Musarion* has nothing Greek about it except the name; even the clothes seem to be eighteenth century.[2] *Die Abderiten* is simply a satire on general human failings, put nominally into Greek dress, in order to add interest and to veil the objectives of the poisoned shafts. It too has no local colour at all. Wieland's later works fall outside my period.[3]

Die Grazien expounds, in allegorical form, Wieland's views on Greek art. He tells how the Graces came to earth to bring to men that extra quality which turns mere earthly beauty into the ideal beauty that the Greeks shed over their works. "Fine young naked maidens breathing sensual desire are not to be taken as Graces. They can be exalted to that level; but such an apotheosis can only be brought about by the imagination of an Apelles."[4] This ideal quality, as Wieland lets us see it, is so utterly un-Greek, so

[1] See F. J. Schneider, *Zwischen Barock und Klassizimus*, p. 240.

[2] "Ein Halstuch öffnet sich, ein Armel fällt zurück."

[3] *Alceste* is particularly interesting for the student of Goethe, as it inspired *Götter, Helden und Wieland* and also foreshadows much of Goethe's practice in *Iphigenie*.

[4] Wieland's *Werke*, Ed. Gruber, Leipzig, 1819, Vol. XII, p. 71.

completely and unashamedly Rococo and French, that we should not be justified in regarding *Die Grazien* as dealing at all with Greek art, did not Wieland expressly state in the introduction that his Graces are Greek and not French.[1]

And what was this quality? An intelligent person of to-day might guess long in vain. For—can it be credited?—it was nothing else than "sex appeal!" Before the Graces came, the shepherdesses of Arcadia were fair indeed, but had "keine Reizungen."

> "Sie wussten nicht
> Wie man einen Blumenstrauss
> Mit Vorteil an den Busen steckt;
> Damit, durch eine kleine List,
> Die Hälfte, die er nicht bedeckt,
> Mehr als das Ganze ist." [2]

The Graces themselves are the super film-stars. "What shall I call you? how express the full sweetness and seduction conveyed by your glances, your smiles, your whole being?" [3] Even when they reveal themselves in their divine form, they breathe out a "nameless attraction." And Venus, their mother, goddess of love, is said to have represented for the Greeks the highest conception of beauty. For Greece of the decadence perhaps, but not for fifth-century Athenians.

If for a moment we escape from sex-appeal, Wieland's ideal of beauty, which, in this essay at least, he genuinely thinks to be the Greek ideal, never rises

[1] *Ibid.*, p. 71. The frequent references to Winckelmann also make it clear that Wieland is thinking primarily of Greek art.

[2] P. 121.

[3] In the edition of 1819 this sentence appears in the form of a verse from which the word "seduction" (Liebreiz) is missing. I quote here from the edition of 1772.

above the "tender" and the "refined," and usually not above the "lovely," the "sweet" and the "delicate." A young Bacchus represents the fairest manly form for him, a youth who has just reached "the borders of the desire-breathing spring-time of eternal youth." Here he had more excuse for being utterly bound by the ideas and tastes of his time, for even Winckelmann had fallen victim. The author of the *Geschichte der Kunst* could never rid himself of that love of the "dainty and refined," as Walter Pater would say, which allowed him to worship the Apollo Belvedere and even to suggest that the ideal was most nearly found in the bodies of castrati and hermaphrodites.[1] This preference of refined softness to robust strength was present also in Goethe's classicism. It was the point on which the Rococo seduced even its greatest enemies.

Die Grazien contained Wieland's ideas on Greek art, but it gave no picture of Greek life. In *Agathon* Wieland drew a detailed and careful picture of Greek civilisation in the fourth century before Christ. He did his best to make an accurate picture according to his knowledge and the ideas he had of the Greeks.[2] Of course, the problems discussed are those of his own day, and they occupy the greater part of the book. But the reader is never left too long without a glimpse of the antique background against which the very modern hero moves and feels. The description of Athens and the Athenians in the eighth book is vividly done, and sound enough, if a little highly

[1] See *Geschichte der Kunst*, Bk. IV, Ch. 2.

[2] See the preface to the first edition. He has tried, he says, to reproduce all the peculiarities of the time and place which he is describing, even to the extent of distinguishing between the habits and characters of Athenians, Ionians and Achaeans.

coloured. But other glimpses show us a world in which it is less easy to recognise ancient Hellas. It is Hellas seen through a pair of bad French binoculars, a Louis XV world of delicate, superficial sensuality, in which " die Grazien " are the supreme divinities.[1]

Agathon's relations to Danae are played throughout against this background. We get the clearest sight of it in the singing contest between Muses and Syrens (Book V, Chapter 5) and in the scene in Hippias' garden,[2] which is worth quoting at length. " Meanwhile a crowd of little cupids and fauns skipped unexpectedly out of the grove. Some were lightly covered in fluttering silver-gauze, in which artificial roses had been twined, others were naked, except for a wreath of ivy and yellow roses, which draped their milky hips. . . . All these little geniuses strewed before Danae the fairest flowers out of pretty little baskets of silver wire. . . . Suddenly the Graces slipped out from behind a myrtle hedge—three young sisters, whose half-unfolded beauty a light mist of silken gauze seemed anxious rather to display than to conceal. They surrounded their mistress, and while the first bound a fresh wreath around her fair brow, the two others kneeling held out to her the choicest fruits and refreshments in golden bowls. At the same time the fauns crowned Hippias with ivy, and poured fragrant unguent over his bald pate and grizzled beard."

In this scene and in the description of the singing

[1] Rossel says: "Son Agathon . . . n'est il pas en somme l'Hellénisme à la recette de Paris?" Cf. also Honegger, *Gesch. des französischen Kultureinflusses*, p. 330.

[2] Bk. VI, Ch. 2. It is true the gardens are said to be " in Persian taste," and Hippias is the type of decadent Greek. But it is certainly meant as a faithful description of the garden of a wealthy Greek in the fourth century.

contest Wieland gives us his most typical view of the Greeks, the view which reflected on to them the characteristics of Rococo civilisation. It was, one may say, the basic view in the 'sixties and 'seventies, the view against which Winckelmann, Lessing, Herder and Goethe had all, consciously or unconsciously, to struggle.

But there are traces in *Agathon* of another conception of them, more serious, and tending more towards idealisation after the manner of the followers of Rousseau. The republic of Tarentum, described in the thirteenth book, is an ideal state of " natural men," ruled, or rather gently guided, by a philosopher-king. The inhabitants were " simple in manners, busy, industrious, law-abiding; foes to splendour and extravagance. . . . Haters of the forced, the ingenious, the exaggerated in all things, and lovers of the natural and the fundamental." The arts were not particularly honoured, nor yet totally despised. They lived at peace with their neighbours and with each other. The philosopher, Archytas, had gradually trained them in good ways, until " they seemed to be ruled rather by the strength of custom than by fear of the law." Archytas himself is an interesting figure. "There was something ideal in the mixture of majesty and charm which spread itself over his whole person. . . . He had never had either a glowing imagination or violent passions. Instead of being ruled by his feelings, he always remained master of them." He even had " silent strength." It is the Laocoön-, no longer the Anacreon-type, and shows how far Winckelmann's influence had penetrated even into the strongholds of the Rococo.

But there is a feeling of unreality about this Utopian

republic. It is described without enthusiasm and fails to carry conviction. Wieland's heart was not in it. He loved to idealise the Greeks as much as anyone, but for no qualities of which Rousseau would have approved. Danae is Greece for him, feminine grace and charm and delicacy, and all the civilised artifices with which the Rococo tried to deck out the hollowness of life. "O Danae!" he exclaims at the end of *Die Grazien*, "what a century was this! This age from Pericles to Alexander, never to be forgotten in the annals of mankind! This age of which, more than of any other, one may say that it lay under the dominion of the Graces."

This was the view of the Greeks with which Goethe came in contact in Leipzig, when he was frankly under Wieland's influence. However much he reacted against it in the *Herderzeit*, a conception of the Greeks so general, and so deeply engrained in the public mentality must have left a permanent mark on the final form of his Hellenism.

CONCLUSION

THE general impression left by this survey may well be one of confusion rather than of clarity. It will be well, therefore, to try to present a unified picture of all the tendencies and attitudes of mind which formed the Greek " atmosphere " of Goethe's youth.

The chief ingredient of that atmosphere was ignorance. The effects of the revival of learning in the schools and universities had not had time to soak through to the general public. For the older generation the Greek authors were mere names whose ancient glory had been sadly dimmed by prejudice and abuse. Even to the young they were hardly more than " distant blue hills." But they were hills to which the young lifted up their eyes, and looked for help to come. The old were ignorant and hostile, the young were ignorant and enthusiastic : from neither could a sound judgment be expected.

Ignorance of Greek art was almost complete, largely because a science of archæology, as we know it to-day, did not exist. But little had been done, before Winckelmann, to collect and make available even such facts as did exist. The collections of Montfaucon and Caylus were well known in Germany, but they did not provide in any way a complete view of Greek art. Such absolutely basic works as the Parthenon sculptures were known only by hearsay.

The history of the ancient world was neglected in all the seats of learning except the most up-to-date, and there were no convenient popular histories to fill the gap. In mythology alone was there a continuous tradition of knowledge in the general public.

This black gulf of ignorance was flimsily covered by a film of superficial knowledge, on which a forest of different conceptions grew up and flourished. There was that of Loën and the Moderns, dying now, but still in its decay stifling and warping the green shoots that yearned to draw life from the sun of Hellas. There was Gottsched, divided between loyalty to Boileau and a secret sympathy with the Moderns. There was Wieland's view (a frequent and vigorous weed), that admired the Greeks but saw in them merely idealised reflections of Rococo society. There was the conception, deriving from Fénelon and Rousseau, of the Greeks as natural, unperverted mankind, the innocent dwellers in the childhood of the world. And finally, there was Winckelmann's burning admiration, the plant that held in its bud the flower of Goethe's classicism, the ideal of the moral man, civilised but healthy, who bears in his breast a "great and composed soul" that makes external law unnecessary, and who shows to the world always "a noble simplicity and silent strength."

In the 'sixties of the eighteenth century all these views were struggling together for supremacy. Nor were they always clearly defined one from another, but they merged into each other, borrowed from each other, and distorted each other in the process. The confusion was appalling. To anyone not armed with knowledge of the Greeks both wide and deep, the task of forming a clear idea of them was almost impossible. Goethe's knowledge was confined to a few subjects and even in these was never profound. He based his final view largely on the views of others, partly on intuition. Which was the more valuable guide?

BIBLIOGRAPHY

BERGER, ARNOLD: "Der junge Herder und Winckelmann," from *Studien zur deutschen Philologie*, Halle, 1903.

BRODE: *Die Friedrichs-Universität zu Halle*, Halle, 1907.

BURSIAN, CONRAD: *Geschichte der klassischen Philologie in Deutschland von den Anfängen bis zur Gegenwart*, Munich and Leipzig, 1883.

FEUERBACH: *Uz und Cronegk*, Leipzig, 1866.

GERICKE, THEO.: *J. M. Gesners und J. J. Herders Stellung in der Geschichte der Gymnasialpädagogik*, 1911.

GUNDOLF, FRIEDRICH: *Goethe*, Berlin, 1930.

HAYM, R.: *Herder nach seinem Leben und Werken dargestellt*, Berlin, 1880.

HEREREN: *Historische Schriften*, Vol. VI, "Chr. Gottl. Heyne biographisch dargestellt," Göttingen, 1823.

HERING: *Einfluss des klassischen Altertums an den Bildungsgang des jungen Goethes*, Frankfurt am Main, 1902.

HOTZY: *Studium zu Goethes mythologischen Quellen*, Vienna, 1912.

JUSTI, K.: *Winckelmann und seine Zeitgenossen*, 1898.

KONT, J.: *Lessing et l'antiquité*, Paris, 1894 and 1899.

KORFF, H. A.: *Geist der Goethezeit*, Leipzig, 1930.

KÖRTE: *Das Leben Gleims*, Halberstadt, 1811.

KÖSTER: *Die deutsche Literatur der Aufklärungszeit*, Heidelberg, 1925.

LANSON, G.: *Histoire de la littérature française*, Paris.

MAASS, E.: *Goethe und die Antike*, 1912.

MONTGOMERY, MARSHALL: *Friederich Hölderlin and the German Neo-Hellenic Movement*, Oxford University Press, 1923.

PAULSEN, FRIEDERICH: *Geschichte des gelehrten Unterrichts auf den deutschen Schulen und Universitäten*, Leipzig, 1885.

REMME, KARL: *Die Hochschulen Deutschlands*, Berlin, 1926.

RIGAULT: *Histoire de la querelle des anciens et des modernes*, Paris, 1856.

ROSSEL, V.: *Histoire des relations littéraires entre la France et l'Allemagne*, 1897.

SANDYS, J. E.: *A History of Classical Scholarship*, 3rd ed., Cambridge, 1921.

SCHAUMKELL: *Herder als Kulturhistoriker*, 1901.

SCHMIDT, ERICH: *Lessing*, Berlin, 1909.

SCHNEIDER, F. J.: *Die deutsche Dichtung zwischen Barock und Klassizismus*, Stuttgart, 1924.

STARK, B.: *Handbuch der Archäologie der Kunst*, Leipzig, 1880.

VOELCKER, H.: *Die Stadt Goethes*, Frankfurt am Main, 1932.

WITKOWSKI, G.: *Die Vorläufer der anakreontischen Dichtung in Deutschland*, Leipzig, 1889.

Printed in England at THE BALLANTYNE PRESS
SPOTTISWOODE, BALLANTYNE & CO. LTD.
Colchester, London & Eton